"Dr. Argie has been a significant part of our ministry here at Enon. We understand counseling to be three things:

1. Lay-biblical teaching

2. Pastoral counseling

3. Therapeutic intervention

There are some issues that can be handled on the lay-biblical level, some issues that need pastoral intervention, but then there's some things that require professional therapeutic care. When it comes to therapeutic intervention, Dr. Argie is our Go-To person! She helps bring hope and healing into the lives of many and so we're just grateful to have an opportunity to speak to whomever will listen and we recognized that Dr. Argie is a significant part of the healing in our community. We believe that her book, Courageous Conversation Connect will bless many.

Rev. Dr. Alyn E. Waller, Senior Pastor

Enon Tabernacle Baptist Church

"What can we say about Dr. Argie Allen Wilson." She's such a blessing, but what I most like about her is that she breaks it down for us to easily understand. We don't like to think about asking for help, even when we clearly need help! The blessing of having Dr. Argie on my show is that somebody could be in there car, in the kitchen cooking dinner, but that message is meant for them and God will make sure that they will hear it because she touches you right there, in your core, it gives you that light bulb moment...that Ah-Ha moment that goes off in your spirit! She's a wonderful addition to our show and she is amazing. I know that anyone who reads her new book, Courageous Conversations Connect is in for a real eye-opening experience.

Patty Jackson, Philadelphia WDAS-FM Radio Personality, iHeart Radio

Insightful, Encouraging, Informative, and Knowledgeable. These are just a few of the many attributes of Dr. Argie Allen Wilson. I am so honored to know Dr. Argie. She is a light that empowers people to think, reflect, and choose a path that produces growth and reconciliation. Her dedication to the well-being of others demonstrates her passion to teach and relate to whomever she is speaking. The past few years of working with Dr. Argie has been a tremendous blessing. I know that Courageous Conversations Connect will bless anyone who reads it, assisting them in embarking on their own healing journey of healthy relationships with themselves and others.

Darryl L. Montague
Author & Entrepreneur

I met Dr. Argie Allen Wilson several years ago
when we were both guests on Pennsylvania State
Senator Vince Hughes' radio show Philly Speaks to
discuss the topic of abusive relationships. Dr. Argie
was serving as an expert on couples and family
counseling and I was serving as an expert on
domestic violence. I was immediately impressed by
her deep understanding of intimate partner violence
and marriage and family therapy. Dr. Argie later
started MC'ing the Women Against Abuse iPledge
press conference, raising her powerful voice to
engage the community at large to work together to
address and prevent domestic violence. Dr. Argie
has a unique mix of brilliance and humility that
leads to her continuous growth and change. At the
same time, she has a deep sense of social
responsibility and strives to utilize her God
endowed skills to help transform our
community. The wisdom that is packed in her new
book, Courageous Conversations Connect is a must
read.

Jeannine L. Lisitski, Ph.D.
Executive Director & President
Women Against Abuse, Inc.

Today's technology has opened the way to more
talk, but less honest intimacy and personal
connections. Keeping it to ourselves, especially
when it hurts, only isolates and discourages us. Dr.
Argie Allen Wilson has created an instrument

through her book that will open us up to ourselves and the people who we care about most as well as to the people in our lives who care about us and want to share life with us. These honest and true conversations, especially when we are hurting will break down the isolation while helping us to gain love, support and open a pathway back to a life of living loved and not a life of living alone. COURAGEOUS CONVERSATIONS CONNECT will ease open that door to light and love.

Harry J. Aponte, LCSW, LMST, LMFT
Author of The Person of the Therapist Training Model - Mastering the Use of Self and Bread & Spirit; Clinical Associate Professor, Couple & Family Therapy Department, Drexel University and in Private Practice in Center City Philadelphia

"Courageous Conversations Connect" is a natural and simple guide to not just finding happiness but achieving self-authenticity and joy. This book invites you to get off the sidelines and live life fully, honestly, and courageously—one conversation at a time. So, get ready to go beyond your comfort zone to living your best life with this profoundly relatable yet mind-expanding book.

Marlene F. Watson, Ph.D., LMFT
Author of Facing the Black Shadow, former Chair, Couple & Family Therapy Department, Drexel University and President, Family Process Institute

In a world where most of us struggle with how to have and maintain healthy relationships in our personal and professional lives, *Courageous Conversations Connect* is a **must read**, offering us a pathway to healing.

In her new book, Dr. Argie helps us find our voice, when faced with the option of avoiding hard conversations. Avoidance is not an option with the things that matter most. She masterfully takes the reader on a wellness journey while giving them a weekly call to action to speak up and have courageous conversations that serve to create meaningful, sustainable and significant connections.

This book keeps the reader engaged and moving forward while creating opportunities for new norms and healthier relationships with themselves and others from beginning to end.

Read it, live it and love the new you!

Sheryl Lee Ralph Hughes, Actor, Author and Activist

COURAGEOUS CONVERSATIONS CONNECT

A Pathway to Reset Your Mindset with Intentional
Thoughts from the Inside-Out
By DR. ARGIE J. ALLEN WILSON, Ph.D.

To Angular
wishing you
love & light
DR Argie
12/7/2019

Copyright © 2019 Dr. Argie J. Allen Wilson

ISBN: 978-1-7923-2194-8

All Rights Reserved

Cover and Logo Design by Diona Nicole Murray

Published in Partnership with Precious Seeds Media Group, LLC

For Worldwide Distribution, Printed in the U.S.A.

Library of Congress Cataloging-in-Publications Data, Courageous Conversations Connect: A Pathway to Reset your Mindset with Intentional Thoughts from the Inside-Out, Wilson Allen, Argie J.

If you like this book, tell your friends! For comments, questions and more information about upcoming books and appearances by Dr. Argie J. Allen Wilson, visit www.drargieconnects.com or email us at contactus@connectionsmatterllc.com.

DEDICATIONS

This book is dedicated to God the Creator who is my source and the one who has blessed me with these gifts as my offering to humanity.

I dedicate this book in memory of the phenomenal woman God blessed me with as my mother, who I affectionately called Queen Elizabeth and my father Hildred G. Allen who continues to always be there for me as the best dad a girl could ever have. It is because of these two amazing human beings, that I have developed into the woman I am today.

Finally, I dedicate this book to the love of my life; my husband, best friend, business partner, prayer partner, soulmate and spiritual leader of our family, Morgan E. Wilson Jr. who expects nothing less than greatness from me and inspires me to go beyond the ordinary to the extraordinary while tapping into the highest version of myself. Thank you for encouraging me to reach for the moon, for always cheering me on and for believing that together, we can make a difference on this journey called life. The best is yet to come. You are truly my DKC. Elephant Juice!

ACKNOWLEDGEMENTS It is with heartfelt

appreciation, adoration, love and gratitude that I thank those who have taken this journey with me throughout the many years of my development. You have all been a clear and present contribution to the words that make up this literary composition represented in Courageous Conversations Connect.

To My GRAND-parents: The late Argie and Orvin Kelly, Lillian and Rush Allen and Grandma Lazane, thank you for teaching me the beginnings of my spiritual foundation, for showing me what resilience looks like in this world and for allowing me to stand on your shoulders of greatness.

To My Sisters: Kimberly S. Alston, Kellie L. Terry and Malta Jones and my double-first cousin Deborah Allen-Hopkins, thank you for the gift of sharing our sisterhood. We continue to create new rituals and embrace old ones and I believe that mom and dad are proud of the women we have become. We are truly stronger because we have each other and I am thankful that God blessed me with you as my sisters.

To My Brothers: Quentin W. Terry Sr. and Joey Petty, thank you for stepping into a space as my brothers that allowed me to know what is means to be loved and that you always have my back.

To My Heartbeats: Nicole E. Gross, Morgan B. Alston, Kyler A. L. Grigsby and Quentin W. Terry Jr., thank you for allowing me to be a significant part of your village and for the privilege of helping to raise you all to be the phenomenal women and men you are today. You were all my first heartbeats and I love being your Auntie. And to my beautiful and precocious little niece Joelle Allyce Gross, who was our families' precious gift on Thanksgiving Day, 2018 when my niece Nicole and nephew Tysean Gross brought her into the world; we truly are thankful for the JOY Jojo has deposited into our lives; her smile makes my hearts smile.

To My Family: My aunties and uncles (including the late Samson, Ulysses, Patrick - Baltimore Orioles #18/Lifeline Ministries & Maybelle Kelly; BJ, Phyllis and the late Mildred & Alma Kelly and Ronnie, Ellis and the late Fred & Theola Allen) and all of my cousins, nieces and nephews, thank you for allowing me to be a part of such an amazing family that has taught me what it looks like to love, respect, support, and encourage each other while challenging each other to be our best. And to my sweet Aunt Dot, (Deaconess Dorothy Allen) thank you for the many prayers you sent up for me over the years and for always believing in my greatness and to my uncle Leroy Kelly (Cleveland Browns Running Back #44 and Hall of Fame Inductee of 1994), thank you for modeling strength and humility in the midst of fame.

To My Spiritual Family: Gene Austin Jefferson and Velva Lilly-Jefferson from Philly, thank you both for always holding Morgan & I up in prayer and for affirming us with your love, laughter, guidance and support.

To My BFF, Sands and Soror Melissa Ayers, thank you for always being my ride or die. Our sisterhood and friendship have truly stood the test of time. Your enduring friendship, love and support means the world to me.

To My HU CREW: The Late Monique Parnell Phifer, Kimberly Dantzler (Bestie), Cheryl Pierson, Charlie Lewis Jr., Carl Touchstone, Blonka Winkfield, Crystal Whaley, Bronwyn Coutee and my honorary HU sisters, Esther Ryans, LaTicia White and Sherry Mullens-Laster; I thank you for allowing me to be a part of such an amazing group of friends. Being connected to you all makes me want to be a better version of ME. We are truly friends who have become Framily. Love Is US! To my special sister-friends Francetta Slacum and Tracy Graham, thank you for being there through the ups and downs of life. To Big Jon, thank you being a true friend from day #1 on (HU) campus.

To My Sister-Circle Girlfriends, Lucienne Sparrow Davis, you have been my encouragement and inspiration for over 3 decades. Candy Manning, you are truly the gift that keeps on giving. Thank you both for always be there for me.

To My Mentor and Dear Friend: Dr. Marlene F. Watson (aka, HT2 – Harriet Tubman 2.0) you are truly one of those rare gifts and I am honored to be able to call you my sister-friend. Thank you for teaching me to speak truth to power and for making sure that I know I have everything I need for this journey to greatness.

To My Bonus Daughter: Thank you, Jessica A. Wilson for allowing me the opportunity to be your bonus mom. You are a wonderful, kind and caring human being. I cherish our mother/daughter relationship and look forward to it continuing to grow.

To My Bonus Son: Morgan T. Wilson, you have been such a delight and pleasant surprise since the first day I met you. I continue to be amazed by your growth, intellect, maturity and nurturing spirit at such a young age. I know you will go on to do great things in this world and I am proud to be your bonus mom.

To My Other Bonus Sons: Wishing all of you, love and light as you traverse though this place called life.

To My Clients: Thank you for trusting the process of therapy and for trusting me to accompany you on your healing journey.

To My Mentees: Thank you for allowing me to stretch you in ways that have also stretched me.

To My Illustrious Sorority: Delta Sigma Theta, thank you for allowing me to serve in the spirit of Sisterhood, Scholarship and Service.

To My Enon Church Family: (SAS and Missions) Thank you for my spiritual foundation from a child to adulthood and for your continued love and support. To whom much is given, much is required.

Table Of Contents

CHAPTER 3 114

STAYING HEALTHY IN THE MIDST OF 114

TRANSITIONS 114

FORWARD

Every once in a while, you come across a literary work that is pure, refreshing and authentic while simultaneously calling you into action. Courageous Conversations Connect does just that. It's a must-read game changer that will positively impact your life. It is no secret that life presents us with more questions sometimes then answers. That said, it has been my experience that the answers may be buried deep inside the very elusive conversations that many of us avoid like the plague.

I met Dr. Argie Allen Wilson many years ago when I was launching my Breaking the Silence Conference in Philadelphia which was focused on bringing education, awareness and sensitivity to Mental Health and Wellness issues in our community while shedding the stigma. She was then and continues to be a champion and advocate for individuals and families who struggle with both mental health challenges and every day relationship issues that negatively impact our communities. Dr. Argie and I have worked diligently together for many years fighting for social justice regarding mental wellness for all people, so when she asked me to write this forward, I was honored because I knew that this book would be a difference maker for the masses.

If we think long enough, I'm sure we all know someone who needs to have a courageous conversation with themselves or with someone else. Whether someone has lost a loved one, they're in a job transition, they're going through a divorce and are trying to figure out how to tell their children or they're so depressed that they no longer find joy in the simple pleasures in life; being courageous enough to have that tough conversation may be just what they need to reconnect with themselves or someone else.

This is where Dr. Argie's Courageous Conversations Connect book comes in handy. Over the many years of our friendship, we have had multiple conversations about why people don't talk to each other when it matters most. We've also talked about why we need to be in on-going conversations with ourselves as well, especially when we're at a crossroads or need to make a difficult decision. In one of our many talks, we both concluded that much of it boils down to fear; fear of rejection, fear of loss, fear of retaliation; fear of failure, fear of success or just plain old fear of anything that people don't want to deal with. This book puts to rest your fears and gives you a pathway to reset your mindset so that you can create a new paradigm shift. Reading Courageous Conversations Connect will enable you to give yourself permission to have the necessary conversations with yourself and others to create a healthier you as well as having more intentional, thoughtful and fulfilling relationships.

This is a book that should be in the hands of anyone who is struggling with fear or avoiding having that difficult conversation. It will give you that call to action you need and encourage you on your healing journey with courageous action steps along the way. Not only will you be stronger, but so will your relationships at the end of your process. Read this book and embark on your journey by having Courageous Conversations that Connect. You'll be glad you did!

Senator Vincent J. Hughes (D); PA District 7

Democratic Chair, Senate Appropriations Committee

PREFACE

I am deeply grateful that so many of you have found this book Courageous Conversations Connect, helpful as you embark on your healing journey.

I have learned over the many years of being a therapist as well as being a part of lived and shared experiences personally, professionally, relationally, familially and spiritually, that there are times in our lives when we all need to muster the courage to have difficult talks which I like to call Courageous Conversations. I believe that most times, we are fearful of having these conversations because we are unsure of the outcome and ultimately believe that it will lead to disconnection, cut-offs or loss. In my experience over the years, if we are courageous enough to have the conversation; the outcome more often than not, leads to us connecting with ourselves and the people who matter to us most. These conversations do not have to lead to despair, sadness or disappointment. As a matter a fact, they have the power to lead to quite the opposite; hopefulness, joy and contentment.

Thus, the following can result from reading this book about how Courageous Conversations Connect.

- When Courageous Conversations Connect with ourselves, we emerge as better versions of "us" as a result of engaging in radical self-care.

- When Courageous Conversations Connect with our relationships, we emerge stronger by learning how to speak truth to power while not losing our humility in the process.

- When Courageous Conversations Connect with our spiritual selves during life's transitions, we emerge with a more satisfied and fulfilled life by choosing to let go of the pain and turn it into power.

- When Courageous Conversations Connect with our intention, we emerge with the ability to reset our mindset; ready and excited to live our BEST Lives with promise, power, purpose and abundance.

This is why I have chosen to call this book Courageous Conversations Connect and I am confident that reading it will make a difference in your life as well as in the relationships you value and treasure most.

Enjoy your journey, one Courageous Conversation at a Time!

Dr. Argie J. Allen Wilson, Ph.D.

*Introduction*This book will give you a pathway to your own personal, relational, emotional and spiritual freedom over the course of 52 weeks by offering you more deliberate opportunities to embrace positive thoughts, harness enormous internal energy and recapture intentional affirming messages designed to release negative toxins in your mind, body and spirit. Courageous Conversations Connect will stimulate mental clarity, leading you on a journey towards radical self-care and giving you the opportunity to have and maintain extraordinary relationships with people who want you to WIN.

My intention is that you gain authentic insight into your own thoughtfulness journey, ultimately creating a paradigm shift in the way you view your own unique understanding and expression of thoughts. These thoughts relate to who you are, who you were designed to be and what gifts you were meant to offer this world as you navigate this complex phenomenon called LIFE.

Courageous Conversations Connect was designed for you to read over the course of one year throughout a journey of 52 weeks on Thursdays or whatever day works for you. It is combined with space for you to make journal entries throughout the course of each week. These entries will allow you to compartmentalize your thoughts in a more comprehensive and caring way while having courageous conversations with yourself first and perhaps others along the way. The expectation is that you will journal your way towards healing as you reset your mindset. The goal will also encourage a *Call to Action* after every *Courageous Conversation Connect* process, which is not only intended for you to tap into your deeper thoughts, but should be utilized to get you to act with intentionality while engaging yourself in growing forward.

This process requires that you engage in a dialogue with yourself while envisioning what your BEST LIFE would look like if you actually began living a life of abundance in every way. Most of us get to Thursday and think; if I can just get to TGIF than I will have survived. The goal of reading this book is not for you to just think about Surviving until Friday, but instead, for you to allow yourself to view Thursdays as an opportunity to hit your stride on your way to Thriving.

Thursdays has always been a day of reflection for me because while it's close to the end of the work week for most people, my job as a relationship therapist usually is not over until Saturday afternoon. That said, as you journey with me on some of my most intimate Courageous Conversations, I would like you to consider your own *Courageous Conversation Reflections* and how you can turn the day before Friday into your own, Super Power Day. This will allow you to reset your mindset to epic wins as you prepare to release, relax and rejuvenate in order to step up and into your next level.

Harnessing your own internal Super Power with your thoughts will allow you to SOAR to endless present and real possibilities. In order to achieve this, you must set your intentions to a new destination in your mind first and then create a new belief with the highest expectations of greatness, thankfulness and expression of love for yourself and others. This, is what Courageous Conversations Connect is all about! Are you ready, willing and able? You have nothing to lose and everything to gain so let's do this together...Let Go, Let God and Let's Go...Your Best Life is on its WAY!!!

Chapter 1
Radical Self-Care In Action

Week 1- Courageous Conversations

Courageous Conversation: Be thankful for the ability to have what, by now, you know I like to call courageous conversations. Sometimes we fail in our relationships because we tend to avoid real and authentic conversations while coasting on the surface. Speaking truth to power and saying what is real can be hard. It's also hard to hear someone else's truth that doesn't quite match up with our own.

That said, however painful it may be, God has a way of turning that pain into power. That pink elephant in the room needs to be moved in order for the healing to transform your relationships. True courageous conversations have the ability to do just that; heal and transform.

It may be an intimate partner, children, a best friend, a trusted confidant or colleague who has hurt you. It may also be you, that is in need of forgiveness. You see, it's often easier to identify when someone else has caused us pain, then it is to acknowledge when we are the perpetrators. If we're honest, we all can be guilty of holding others accountable in ways that we are unwilling to hold ourselves accountable for. If you are struggling with simply saying that you were wrong and in need of someone's forgiveness or struggling to share how someone hurt you, this is a great week to embark on a paradigm shift.

Whatever the circumstances, you have a decision to make. You can either, suffer in silence refusing to have the courageous conversation with yourself or someone else which has the potential to keep you stuck in bitterness, resentment and anger or you can take a leap of faith and have the courageous conversation of a lifetime. The choice is yours! If your relationship is on life support or you yourself are feeling a sense of deep pain, you have very little to lose anyway, so why not go for it.

It's been said that resentment, bitterness and unforgiveness is like drinking poison and expecting the other person to die. No one wins in this situation and when we refuse talk about the hurt, injury or pain we feel or resist hearing about someone else's feelings, these emotions have the potential to become cancerous. They tend to fester inside of us turning into toxic waste that spreads like wild fire, preventing us from living the life we were intended to live with joy, purpose and abundance. Having the courage to have these conversations can be a pathway to arresting negative emotions and allowing yourself to tap into emotional freedom.

***Call to Action:** Take a risk with someone you love to have that courageous conversation you've been needing to have for a while. It may be the difference maker in your relationship so go for it. Speak from your heart with "I" statements without blaming or shaming. Focus on simply sharing your heart through your authentic voice and/or be willing to hear from them in their authentic voice. If no one comes to mind, have a courageous conversation with yourself by writing yourself a letter and reflecting on the intentionality of the message. Sometimes, we need to forgive ourselves realizing that the courageous conversation must start, "from ourselves; with ourselves".*

Have a **beautiful day** on purpose from my heart to yours!

Journal Entry Date: _____

Courageous Action #1

_____

_____

_____

_____

Three Reasons Why This Is Significant for My Life:

Reason One: _____

Reason Two:_____

Reason Three:_____

What Will You Do With This Moment That
Allows It To Be Impactful For You and Others:

_____

_____

_____

_____

_____

What Courageous Conversation Can You Create
From This Action: _____

_____

_____

_____

_____

Week 2- Overcoming the Disease to Please

Courageous Conversation: Why do people pleasers end up getting the short end of the stick in upside down relationships?

People pleasers are not just nice people who want to do the right thing or who go overboard trying to make everyone happy. Those who suffer from the disease to please are people who say "Yes" when they really want to say "No" and then regret that they are now committed to participating in something that they have no interest or desire to be a part of.

Here you will find insight and solutions to overcome the disease to please. If you desire to overcome the disease to please, it's important to first learn the art of saying no. First, contrary to popular belief, we have to recognize and accept that no is not a bad word. Second, we have to change the way we think about relationships; the relationship isn't bad just because we get disappointed sometimes or don't always get what we want.

We often say "no" out of fear versus "yes" out of love. What do I mean by that? Well, I'm glad you asked; sometimes we tend to say yes because of fear of *lack* or *loss*. We tend to acquiesce to certain undesirable requests because of our Stinking Thinking, telling ourselves that others won't like us, or that they may reject us, not be friends with us or even leave us. The truth is that there are times when we need to say, "no" out of love for ourselves and perhaps even the other person that we are enabling as they work towards becoming less co-dependent. That "no" to others has the ability to transform into a "yes" for ourselves creating more time, self-care opportunities and balance.

Failure to please ourselves is one of the main byproducts related to people pleasers. It's important to think about preserving yourself before you submit to the urge to please. If you are not compromising yourself then pleasing another may be fine, but if you find yourself often in the one down position, then it's time to re-evaluate your actions. Remember, our healthy relationships are only healthy because we are able to acknowledge our own limitations as well as that of others. Part of being an adult requires that we adapt to change and sometimes disappointment. Sometimes our closest friends and family must learn to accept our limitations. The sooner that we accept our own limitations, the healthier we'll be.

Try to remember when you started being unable or unwilling to say "no", as oppose to setting better boundaries:

- If you can remember when the origin of this behavior started, you may be able to better understand how to stop it.

- If your yeses have gotten you in trouble, make a list of the outcomes related to your people pleasing behavior.

- Then list the alternative potential outcomes, had you not submitted to people pleasing for the wrong reasons.
- Seeing a different outcome may give you a tangible reason to change your behavior.

Our self-esteem must be intact to resist the urge to people please unnecessarily. Remember, there is nothing fundamentally wrong with pleasing people unless we are constantly the casualty in the process. A good way to measure the authenticity of your relationship is to just say no to something requested and see what happens.

We all need to learn to say "no" out of love sometimes versus "yes" out of fear. Don't allow your fear to paralyze you so much that you can't set boundaries when you need to. Remember, people exploit people who don't have healthy boundaries.

People can never fill up on the outside what needs to be filled up on the inside. Ask yourself the question; if this person never speaks to me again because I said no, are they deserving of the relationship anyway?

Call to Action: If you find yourself always compromising your integrity for someone specifically, then it's important to discern the integrity of that relationship. Re-evaluating the cost to your soul & spirit will help you to determine if the cost of people pleasing has become too high. List the number of times you have found yourself saying "yes" to something you wanted to say "no" to, only to regret it later. Draw a line connecting the act to what it cost you (i.e. sleep, money, friendships, your mental or physical health etc.). This may help you set better boundaries. Also, don't say "yes" right away; say you'll think about it. This will give you time to process if you really want to commit or not. Remember, folks who can't or won't accept your "no" might be undeserving of your "yes".

Have a **beautiful day** on purpose from my heart to yours!

Journal Entry Date: _____

Courageous Action #2

_____

_____

_____

_____

Three Reasons Why This Is Significant for My Life:

Reason One: _____

Reason Two:_____

Reason Three:_____

What Will You Do With This Moment That
Allows It To Be Impactful For You and Others:

_____

_____

_____

_____

_____

What Courageous Conversation Can You Create
From This Action: _____

_____

_____

_____

_____

Week 3-Making a Difference

Courageous Conversation: Have you ever wondered why some days feel really great when we've embarked on a random act of kindness? Ask yourself when is the last time you did something for someone that wasn't out of obligation or responsibility.

Just having another day to make a difference in someone's life can go a long way not just for them but for ourselves as well and it cost us nothing. The saying goes; to the world you may be one person, but to one person you may be the world. If our daily desire was to be the world to one person through encouragement, words of affirmation, and empowering folks to live their best lives, think how much of a difference we would all make here on this planet.

Sometimes we may feel that we have very little to offer, yet some of the most valuable things in life are free. Smiles are a universal language that doesn't cost us anything; carrying an elderly person's bags across the street might take less than a minute but create a lifetime of gratitude; or a quick call or text just to say I'm thinking about you has the power to brighten someone's day and perhaps give them hope to fight another day. These are just a few things that we can do as a collective to make a difference in our communities. The possibilities are infinite and all you have to do is offer your gift of caring.

Call to Action: Join me in offering someone a word of encouragement, affirmation and appreciation today. It feels so much better to speak life into others through the light of word, deed and action. You may be pleasantly surprised at how your random act of kindness not only helps someone else but sews into your life as well.

Have a **beautiful day** on purpose from my heart to yours!

Journal Entry Date: _____

Courageous Action #3

_____

_____

_____

_____

Three Reasons Why This Is Significant for My Life:

Reason One: _____

Reason Two:_____

Reason Three:_____

What Will You Do With This Moment That
Allows It To Be Impactful For You and Others:

_____

_____

_____

_____

_____

What Courageous Conversation Can You Create
From This Action: _____

_____

_____

_____

_____

Week 4- The Gift of Life

Courageous Conversation: Each day we wake up, we have another opportunity to either count every day or make every day count! Why do we often choose the former as though making every day count is not an option?

Do you find yourself getting paralyzed with negative thoughts that only focus on what you don't have versus what you do have? Sometimes life can get pretty overwhelming with our continuous **to-do lists, more month than money and more tasks than time.** That said, each day that we get another spin around the sun offers us hope that there is still time to enjoy our journey. When I'm fretting about certain things that I have no control over, I remember to be thankful for my life and the endless possibilities to live in abundance by simply choosing JOY. This allows me to focus on what I do have versus what I don't have.

It's not so complicated; because I woke up, God has given me another opportunity to live life to its' fullest and sense my time is short on this planet, I figure that I might as well make it count. How about you? You can choose to enjoy this journey we call life or get stuck in regrets from the past, worry in the present or fear of the unknown future. I say, let's start today with appreciating the most important gift of all, your LIFE. You only get one here on earth and there are no dress rehearsals so get off the sidelines and get in the game.

Call to Action: Are you guilty of focusing on the negative aspects of your life? If so, are you open to a new paradigm shift by taking all of the lessons learned from your past mistakes and harnessing them as an opportunity to share, love, give and enjoy your life with human touchpoints. List your mistakes, and what you learned from them. Then, make a list of ways to use those lessons as gifts to help someone else. By doing this, you simply make a decision to give humanity the best gift you have to offer, YOU! Remember, what you put out into the universe will not return void. Embrace YOUR BEST LIFE in Abundance NOW!

Have a **beautiful day** on purpose from my heart to yours!

Journal Entry Date: _____
Courageous Action #4

_____

_____

_____

_____

Three Reasons Why This Is Significant for My Life:
Reason One: _____

Reason Two:_____

Reason Three:_____

What Will You Do With This Moment That
Allows It To Be Impactful For You and Others:

_____

_____

_____

_____

_____

What Courageous Conversation Can You Create
From This Action: _____

_____

_____

_____

_____

Week 5- Speak L.I.F.E.
Words of Love, Integrity, Freedom
and Energy

Courageous Conversation: Have you ever thought about the opportunity we all have to speak either life or death into people? It's really our choice!

The power of words, matter and we can speak life into ourselves and others with one decision to lift up versus put down. In a world where we are encouraged to not be kind and affirming to others, while highlighting the worst of someone's limitations, titanic plates can shift with one decision to use words to help and not hurt those we encounter daily. Besides, it takes much more energy to be mean spirited than kind spirited. My mother used to say, it's nice to be important, but it's more important to be nice.

Ask yourself this question; Are your words, actions or deeds **helping to harm or healing the hurt**? If you answered yes to the former, there is still time to right the ship. Make a decision to use your words for good, not evil; for affirmation not degradation; to cast light not darkness and to make a difference versus contributing to chaos, disruption and despair. You won't regret making a decision to take action to embark on the journey of healing. You can make this world better simply because you made a decision to SPEAK LIFE!

Call to Action: Let's embark on a healing journey to speak words of life into each person you connect with daily and see how your words of kindness, inspiration, aspiration, motivation and spiritual elevation come back to you in the divine universal laws of CONNECTION.

Have a **beautiful day** on purpose from my heart to yours!

Journal Entry Date: _____

Courageous Action #5

_____

_____

_____

_____

Three Reasons Why This Is Significant for My Life:

Reason One: _____

Reason Two:_____

Reason Three:_____

What Will You Do With This Moment That
Allows It To Be Impactful For You and Others:

_____

_____

_____

_____

_____

What Courageous Conversation Can You Create
From This Action: _____

_____

_____

_____

_____

Week 6- Celebrate Life on Purpose

Courageous Conversation: Have you ever wondered why we only celebrate our Birthdays once a year, when in reality we wake up with breath in our bodies every day?

What if we made a decision to celebrate our lives every day, 365 days a year? What if we looked at the fact that we woke up as another opportunity to live our best lives now? Each day that we get to experience life is a reminder of love, light, truth and accountability that ultimately equals hope and freedom. These truths connect with the spirit of goodness. Although, it may not always feel like it, the truth is that we get to write our own story if we are courageous enough to access the power that is within us. We are already game changers and difference makers and it is our birthright that has come from our inheritance that informs our greatness. We have the ability to create our own narrative from the place of power and wholeness.

Even though that sounds great, you may feel like your struggles are insurmountable and that someone else is writing your story. It's important to not give others the power to create a narrative about your story that doesn't fit your reality. If you do, it may mean you have ultimately given your Super Powers away. Remember, just waking up reminds us that we have not arrived at the end of our destination. There are still chapters in our story yet to be written and the best is yet to come.

Call to Action: Make a decision to Celebrate Your Life and all the good that it has to offer humanity on purpose! What does this mean? Start putting pen to paper and begin to re-write your script. Make sure the you write your story exactly the way that you want it to be told. Remember, you have the power to honor old chapters of your life by bringing closure to the past and embracing the present while looking forward to the further. Be intentional about creating new chapters that speak to your authentic journey while celebrating your life with passion, power & purpose!

Have a **beautiful day** on purpose from my heart to yours!

Journal Entry Date: _____

Courageous Action #6

_____

_____

_____

_____

Three Reasons Why This Is Significant for My Life:
Reason One: _____
Reason Two:_____
Reason Three:_____

What Will You Do With This Moment That
Allows It To Be Impactful For You and Others:

_____

_____

_____

_____

_____

What Courageous Conversation Can You Create
From This Action: _____

_____

_____

_____

_____

Week 7- Increase Your Territory

Courageous Conversation: What's next…have you done all there is to do or do you have something left in the tank for the next leg of the journey?

Sometimes we need to be thankful for the gift of having our territory increased. Like the prayer of Jabez, I know that God has plans to increase my territory. I'm not even sure what that looks like but I know as sure as my name is Dr. Argie, that the blessings are on the way both to the giver and the receiver. I ask God daily, who will you have me to touch today and who will I be touched by. What about you? Try asking God that question and see how he blesses you to be a blessing.

We don't always think that we are ready to expand our reach, but our lived and shared experiences are what ultimately connects us to humanity. If you have had some bumps and bruises along the way, those battles scars may be just the stripes you need for your next assignment. Everything that we've been through has prepared us to live our lives and play full out on purpose. So, the next time you think you're not ready for your territory to be increased, take a walk down memory lane and trace your steps highlighting how far you've come and who you've touched along the way. You may be surprised when you realize that you don't look like what you've been through and your journey has not been in vein. There is more that is desired of you so let go, let God and let's go.

Call to Action: Embrace the enhancement of your territory and look forward to the intersection of lived and shared experiences with others. Make a decision to show up and show out on purpose. List those you are able to lift up, affirm and support. Focus on expanding your gifts, talents and treasures to those in need. As your territory is increased, you will experience what being blessed to be a blessing looks like in action.

Have a **beautiful day** on purpose from my heart to yours!

Journal Entry Date: _____

Courageous Action #7

_____

_____

_____

_____

Three Reasons Why This Is Significant for My Life:

Reason One: _____

Reason Two:_____

Reason Three:_____

What Will You Do With This Moment That
Allows It To Be Impactful For You and Others:

_____

_____

_____

_____

_____

What Courageous Conversation Can You Create
From This Action: _____

_____

_____

_____

_____

Week 8- Rejuvenate Your life!

Courageous Conversation: Do you ever feel as though you aren't getting anywhere in life? Do you wonder if time is passing you by or why it's taking so long for you to achieved your goals, wishes and dreams? What about feeling that others are exceeding you in their accomplishments and that you're being left behind. Sound familiar?

Well, if this sounds like the thoughts inside your head, you may need to *Rejuvenate Your Life* in order to start feeling positive and alive again. It's never good to play the comparison game. If you feel like others are exceeding you, then it's time to level up your focus on yourself. It's been said that if the grass seems greener on the other side of the street, then it's time to water your own grass. Focusing on what others have accomplished versus yourself, won't help you get to where you want to be. The difference in where you are and where you want to be is YOU! You are the common denominator. Changing your thought process and re-directing those energies onto and into you with a positive perspective is key. This change will require a radical shift in order to reset your mindset.

Sometimes we need to figure out how to nurture our relationship with ourselves. Additionally, in a world where we are constantly required to pour out on our jobs, in our families, in our communities etc., we need to find those who are ready, willing and able to pour into us. And if that's not an option, then we must take action to rescue ourselves with the acts of revitalization, restoration and rejuvenation.

Time to take action to recharge your emotional and relational battery, re-establish healthy connections with those in your life who are willing to have reciprocal relationships with you. Then, begin the process of rejuvenating your mind, body and spirit so that you can get back in the game of life. Changing your mindset is possible, and I'm sure you are capable, now you just have to decide if you are willing. Time to start enjoying the life you want, desire, deserve and were designed to live on purpose.

Call to Action: It's time to put your **Oxygen Mask** on first and prioritize yourself. Remind yourself that taking care of YOU is not an act of selfishness; it's an act of self-preservation.

Make a list of things you can do to rejuvenate your mind, body and spirit. List what you would like to accomplish and list the action steps necessary to assist you in accomplishing your goals, wishes and dreams. Then make a commitment to do one thing on your list every week until you have finished one goal or accomplishment and then proceed to the next. Even though it may be difficult, it will be exciting to work towards completion of your achieving your goals and aspirations. Your rejuvenated life is in your hands so go for it!

Have a **beautiful day** on purpose from my heart to yours!

Journal Entry Date: _____

Courageous Action #8

_____

_____

_____

_____

Three Reasons Why This Is Significant for My Life:

Reason One: _____

Reason Two:_____

Reason Three:_____

What Will You Do With This Moment That
Allows It To Be Impactful For You and Others:

_____

_____

_____

_____

_____

What Courageous Conversation Can You Create
From This Action: _____

_____

_____

_____

_____

Week 9- Nurturing Your Relationship with Yourself

Courageous Conversation: Have you ever wondered why we often expect others to treat us better than we treat ourselves?

We teach people how to treat us. Reciprocity often fosters healthier relationships because both parties can be active participants. Find effective ways to treat yourself well. Once you list those *treat yourself well* activities, practice them daily. Make a decision to friend yourself.

Identify ways you are a good friend to someone else, then implement similar things that honor friending you.

Remember, if you do what you always did, you'll get what you always got. Make a list of things you used to do and don't do anymore or things you wish to do but are too afraid to do. Find an accountability partner to keep you focused on trying new things.

Focus on simply saying thank you. Accepting simple compliments can go a long way for developing your self-esteem. Identify things you like about yourself and be intentional about complimenting yourself. Internalizing positive words of affirmation can go a long way. Some examples:

- Being the best, allows me to be the best with others!
- My destiny involves my greatness!
- Taking care of me is the best thing I can do for me and you!
- I am worthy of all that God has for me!
- To not live up to my full potential is to deny God's true design for my life!
- Choosing joy in my life allows me to live my best life!
- Today, I will focus on what I have to offer vs what I don't have to offer!
- Tomorrow is just another opportunity to live a great life!

Engage in thought substitution when negative thoughts over power you.

If you hang out with folks who support negative behaviors or are verbally-emotionally abusive toward you, you may need to re-evaluate your crew. If the folks you hang out with are always negative or abusive this could be keeping you sick. Don't keep folks who are unhealthy beyond their expiration date.

Don't dumb yourself down because you're fearful of success or failure. Know that you are a work in progress and the outcome of your hard work on you is going to be an awesome blessing to humanity. We are all under construction but the goal is not to abandon the project before it's completion. When you believe you're worthy of greatness it's half the battle.

Why wait for someone else to do something nice for you when you can take care of it yourself. Treat yourself well and do something nice for you because you deserve it. Remember, nothing is constant but change. Don't run away from making changes to live a better life. You won't regret nurturing the relationship with yourself and those you are closest to well catch your overflow of positive energy.

***Call to Action:** List your 5 top changes that will help you to nurture yourself. Then list 5 steps for each change that will help you to move towards living your best life.*

The greatest gift you can give to your present or future partner/ relationships is to be a healthier well nurtured you. If you don't engage in developing a healthier you, then you will take your unhealthy self, right into your unhealthy relationships!

Have a **beautiful day** on purpose from my heart to yours!

Journal Entry Date: _____

Courageous Action #9

_____

_____

_____

_____

Three Reasons Why This Is Significant for My Life:

Reason One: _____

Reason Two:_____

Reason Three:_____

What Will You Do With This Moment That
Allows It To Be Impactful For You and Others:

_____

_____

_____

_____

_____

What Courageous Conversation Can You Create
From This Action: _____

_____

_____

_____

_____

Week 10- Your Ability to See Clearly

Courageous Conversation: Sometimes it's difficult for us to see the forest for the trees. Clarity comes from the inside-out. If we are operating with blurred vision, we may need to change our viewpoint in order to see more clearly.

I'm thankful for the ability to see clearly. I think the song goes; I can see clearly now the rain is gone; I can see all obstacles in my way. Well, I know that my life, nor yours is not designed as a straight path with no obstacles. Our lives have been designed by God to withstand all the twists and turns, ups and downs, trials and tribulations, appointments and disappointments. This is all a part of our lived and shared experiences in humanity. That said, it's soooo much better if you don't have to face those obstacles blindly when they come. No one likes to be blindsided. Being blindsided often leaves us feeling even more confused and unclear. Yet, when we are able to see more clearly, this allows us the ability to understand how to navigate life's challenges more effectively. The miracle is that there is always a lesson to be learned from the journey when we have clear lenses to see through. So, if you need new lenses, make a decision to change your view point from the inside out to bring clarity to the next stage of your life.

Call to Action: Think about developing clear lenses to help you to see your way through obstacles both internally and externally. Join me in using lessons learned to prepare for the next journey that's bound to have obstacles. Always remember, it may be a different issue but it's always the same God! Whatever obstacle we face is nothing that God plus you or I can't grow through!

Have a **beautiful day** on purpose from my heart to yours!

Journal Entry Date: _____

Courageous Action #10

_____

_____

_____

_____

Three Reasons Why This Is Significant for My Life:

Reason One: _____

Reason Two:_____

Reason Three:_____

What Will You Do With This Moment That
Allows It To Be Impactful For You and Others:

_____

_____

_____

_____

_____

What Courageous Conversation Can You Create
From This Action: _____

_____

_____

_____

_____

Week 11- Rejuvenate Your Social Life

Courageous Conversation: Have you ever wondered why some people have very active social lives and others seem to struggle in developing a satisfying social life?

Just like anything else, creating social connections take work. There is an art to creating a spark in your social life. If you find that you are bored all the time and that the things you used to enjoy you don't find enjoyable anymore then, perhaps it's time to focus on the new you with new interests. If it's fear that's keeping you stuck; remember that fear is only a barrier if you allow it to be.

Practice asking one new person to go to an event each month. Don't be afraid to go to events solo; you never know who you might meet. Going to events solo opens up new liberating opportunities to meet different people and can be very liberating. Remember, every life cycle stage offers different challenges with different solutions. Make sure that your activities are congruent with your age, social circumstances and life cycle stage. Hanging with negative people is never good for your social life. Start trying to diversify your group of friends and begin hanging out with a more positive crew. Don't be afraid or feel like you're disloyal if you start developing new acquaintances that have similar interests. As long as your interests are not harming anyone and you are making you a priority, then it may lead to you to be happier and more connected.

Call to Action: The development of our social lives is really our responsibility, not anyone else's. Whether, your social life has been challenged due to life circumstances such as death, divorce, job loss, relocation etc., you can rejuvenate it but it will take time and work. Be patient with yourself. Create opportunities to improve your social life by taking action to connect with positive friends, acquaintances or just with you. Make a decision to participate in activities, social events and target rich environments once a week. Enjoy Rejuvenating Your Social Life!

Have a **beautiful day** on purpose from my heart to yours!

Journal Entry Date: _____

Courageous Action #11

_____

_____

_____

_____

Three Reasons Why This Is Significant for My Life:

Reason One: _____

Reason Two:_____

Reason Three:_____

What Will You Do With This Moment That
Allows It To Be Impactful For You and Others:

_____

_____

_____

_____

_____

What Courageous Conversation Can You Create
From This Action: _____

_____

_____

_____

_____

Week 12- Smile; Your Best Life is Depending on IT

Courageous Conversation: Have you ever wondered why it takes less energy to smile then to frown. Smiles change the atmosphere from the inside out. It often sets the tone for a positive connection versus a negative connection which has the propensity to reset your mindset.

I'm thankful for just waking up with a smile on my face. I smile simply because I'm here. Waking up means I have another opportunity to make a difference in someone's life. I hope to do just that because my being here is for the purpose of serving others. If you're reading this that means you woke up too, so make a difference at the very least by putting a smile on someone's face. When you smile at them and they smiled back at you, you have made a connection. Smiles are our universal language and we are tailor made to be that light to someone else every day.

I'm not suggesting that you smile when you sad, angry or even disappointed. But I am suggesting that when you focus on what you have to be grateful for, you can usually find at least one thing out of many that has the potential to spark a smile inside of you. Even thinking about a future pregnant with possibilities can be enough for you to smile even in the midst of your present circumstances.

Call to Action: *Make a decision that no matter what's going on in your life, you are going to make every day precious by being thankful that you woke up with a smile. Take that smile and give it away as a gift to someone else and you might be pleasantly surprised at what comes back to you.*

Have a **beautiful day** on purpose from my heart to yours!

Journal Entry Date: _____

Courageous Action #12

_____

_____

_____

_____

Three Reasons Why This Is Significant for My Life:

Reason One: _____

Reason Two:_____

Reason Three:_____

What Will You Do With This Moment That
Allows It To Be Impactful For You and Others:

_____

_____

_____

_____

_____

What Courageous Conversation Can You Create
From This Action: _____

_____

_____

_____

_____

Week 13- Embarking on Your Next Level

Courageous Conversation: Have you ever had a transformative experience that caused you to act, look, feel, talk and be different?

It was my 3rd time visiting Nairobi, Kenya and each time I returned from the Mother Land, my light was brighter and I had a more determined spirit within me than ever. I dare say none of us on the Enon mission team returned to America the same way we left. Perhaps it was the sweet spirit of the children who were polite, kind and respectful. They walked for miles to school with no food in their bellies and no shoes on their feet, yet all they wanted to do was be educated. They asked for pencils and paper versus candy like most children would typically ask for. Or perhaps my transformation was connected to my engagement with our Kenyan brothers and sisters who always greeted us with beautiful smiles offering us bread and chai simply to say thank you for coming. This was all that they had and they were willing to share it with us. It made me think about whether I would share my last drink if I had none left for myself. How about you?

Sometimes we need life altering experiences to remind us of how blessed we truly are and to shift us into action. I became more determined than ever to do, say and be whatever God wanted me to do, say and be. What is your transformative experience and how has it shifted you into action to go to your next level?

Call to Action: *Be thankful that even though you may not be where you want to be, you are not where you use to be either. Every day gives you another opportunity to embark on your next level. People don't plan to fail; they fail to plan. So, the question is, when the opportunity comes your way, will you be prepared, ready and able to go to your next level? Don't detour when God is expecting you to follow through on the next-level plan for your life! You will not only be blessed, but you will be a blessing. All you need to do is stay focused and don't quit. Your Next Level is waiting for you!*

Have a **beautiful day** on purpose from my heart to yours.

Journal Entry Date: _____

Courageous Action #13

_____

_____

_____

_____

Three Reasons Why This Is Significant for My Life:
Reason One: _____
Reason Two:_____
Reason Three:_____

What Will You Do With This Moment That
Allows It To Be Impactful For You and Others:

_____

_____

_____

_____

_____

What Courageous Conversation Can You Create
From This Action: _____

_____

_____

_____

_____

CHAPTER 2
The Cost of Love: How to WIN Regarding Money, Sex and Kids in Your Relationship

The Cost of Love: & Money

Here we explore the **Role of Money** in Relationships. Money and Power - who controls what and how people use their power can be a significant contributor to a healthy or unhealthy relationship.

- How does a spender and a saver get along?
- Teaching kids about the value of money
- Financial Abuse (spending addiction)
- Learning to combine your finances as a healthy couple

Week 14-Money & Power: Who Controls What?

Courageous Conversation: Have you ever felt that your partner wants to control the purse strings in the relationship? Maybe your feeling is real.

Let's talk about balancing your agreement so that money becomes a vehicle for healthy living, not a competition related to hierarchy. If your partner has no sense of finances and appropriate boundaries when it comes to saving, you may need to have a conversation about spender-saver characteristics in relationships.

Ask them do they want to just survive or thrive? Opposites attract, but can they live together in financial harmony when it comes to saving and spending? Conflicting money management styles for spenders and savers can make for uncomfortable friction. I'll share some simple strategies, for spenders and savers to get along financially.

Spenders

- Tend to have very few boundaries when it comes to last minute purchases.
- Will spend now and worry later.
- Will want you as the friend or partner to spend regardless of the consequences.
- Will tend to have the characteristic of buyer's remorse.

Savers

- Savers tend to be thinkers about the consequences.
- Savers are often frugal and hold themselves accountable to stick to their budget.
- Savers often have control issues regarding rigid ways to execute on finances.
- Savers tend to me more rigid and less flexible regarding the execution of finances.

Conflict

- If you are a saver paired with a spender as a partner and/or a friend you may find yourself making purchases that are in congruent to your ideology or your budget.

Keep in mind that at the end of the day the bill is yours to pay, not your friends or your partners who may be excited at the very notion of a purchase regardless of the consequences.

Compromise

- If you and your partner land on opposite ends of the spectrum, try to embrace what you both bring to the table that helps you to grow and stretch. Embrace your differences and similarities. Make them work for you as a couple versus against you.

Early Communication

- When we are in the dating process, it's important to pay attention to whether your partner is a saver or spender. The very thing that might turn you on (i.e. spontaneous spending), might be the very thing that leads you to the poor house if you are married with children. Communicating early and often about management of finances is key.

Contribution

- It can be a blessing to a relationship if the spender can learn from the saver and the saver can learn from the spender. These lessons have utility fostering the ability for both parties to feel valued and not judged. This allows each party to make valid contributions to the management of the money.

Commitment

- If you don't see eye to eye regarding your finances try to think about the models that you had versus your partner; it may help you to understand why your ideologies are so different and help you to co-create a financial style that works for your collective system.

Common Ground

- Don't give up! Remember that you can find some common ground with regards to your finances. Common ground regarding your finances may require time, professional insight perhaps with a financial advisor and a willingness to step outside of your comfort zone.

Connection

- Stay Connected with the process of growing your financial muscles. Be patient with your progress and remember to celebrate your financial wins collectively.

Call to Action: Remember that money is a powerful thing in a relationship. Don't allow money to hold the power in your relationship. Have monthly financial meetings to evaluate how you are doing with your money agreements and to make sure everyone is on the same page. Regain your power by staying connected to each other and the process so that everybody WINS.

Have a **beautiful day** on purpose from my heart to yours!

Journal Entry Date: _____

Courageous Action #14

_____

_____

_____

_____

Three Reasons Why This Is Significant for My Life:

Reason One: _____

Reason Two:_____

Reason Three:_____

What Will You Do With This Moment That
Allows It To Be Impactful For You and Others:

_____

_____

_____

_____

_____

What Courageous Conversation Can You Create
From This Action: _____

_____

_____

_____

_____

Week 15-Teaching Kids About the Value of Money

Courageous Conversation: As an adult, what's the one thing you know for sure about *money*? That it's a limited resource.

In this entry we'll discuss how to **teach your kids the value of a dollar.** Teaching your kids these fundamental rules about money will go a long way when they become young adults.

Money Rules to Live by....

- You can still live below your means while still enjoying life.
- Don't spend more than you make, it's simple arithmetic.
- If you can't afford it don't buy it.
- Learn the art of delayed gratification.
- Good debt is cheaper and gets you something (i.e. a house, education or building a business etc.)
- Bad debt can cost you everything, especially things you can't put a price tag on like peace and harmony in your relationships.
- Declare financial independence by investing in yourself for the future (i.e. pay yourself first through saving).
- Don't loan money to friends or family; this is an easy way to lose them when they don't pay you back. It's better that you determine an amount you can afford as a gift.

- Don't borrow what you can't payback.
- If you can't pay it back then have an honest conversation with the lender about when you can honor your agreement.
- Reset your mindset with money which will help you save more than you spend.

A great lesson to learn and teach your kids is that setting financial boundaries with yourself means saying no to lots of things you want right now but need to wait until later. The cost of setting financial boundaries may render you more gains then you actually realize.

If you find yourself having difficulty paying all the bills and meeting all the needs and wants of your kids, perhaps you need to re-evaluate what funds you have coming in and going out. List all the things you purchase for yourself, family and kids that are a need and those things that are wants. Have a talk with your kids about needs versus wants and have a family agreement to minimize everyone's wants collectively. Wants are related to things that we as humans want to acquire versus needs which are related to the things, we as humans actually need to survive. If you don't make this distinction, you may find yourself only surviving when your ultimate goal is for you and your family to embark on thriving.

Remember, years ago our grandparents who raised their kids during a depression learned how to save more then they spent. We must remember that the highs and lows of our economy impacts us all. We can no longer act like our money habits don't affect our families and our kids. Just start by having a talk with your children about ways that everyone can help save money. Approach your familial shift in spending habits like a team project; everyone has to chip in and participate in the change. Once the money shift has taken root, then celebrate by creating a family ritual that honors your savings. Talking about money should be normalized so that everyone in the family becomes more comfortable. Holding your partner and your kids accountable for staying within the budget will help the family stay on track.

Sometimes, a healthy "no" to that shopping trip, that night out for dinner or even that cup of expensive coffee on the way to work can make a big difference. Just saying no to your own guilty pleasures might help to show your kids that you're willing to make changes too.

Remember, you are not helping your kids if you send them the message that they can have everything they want regardless of their needs. A wonderful virtue to teach your kids is the value of *patience* and working towards *earning* the things you want.

Develop a budget for your kids where they put their allowance into three categories: savings, spending and charity. Finding ways to share in family giving by supporting a charity or worthy cause is a great way to feel good about spending. Create a family agreement regarding how much you are able and/or willing to spend. Remember, more is often caught than taught when it comes to kids. Your kids will model bad spending habits if you demonstrate them regularly and are more likely to model good spending habits even if it's due to a stern financial course correction.

Patterns are powerful because they have been a part of folks lives longer than we all realize. They take root and become cycles difficult to break if we are unaware of them.

Don't just pay attention to the patterns; go one step further and pay attention to the origin of those patterns. Where did you learn them and who taught you these patterns? Then the question is...do you want to keep these patterns or do you want to change them because they render such negative consequences. If your negative spending patterns are not working for you or your kids, it's time to make a change for your families' sake.

Call to Action: If you learned poor spending habits you can change your habits but it will take work on everyone's part, so let's go for it!

List three poor spending habits that you do and you also see your kids do.

Have a conversation with kids and list 3 more positive spending habits that might help you and kids to shift. Choose an accountability partner in the family that will help you with your goal.

List 3 things you can substitute your spending with instead and then share this with your families' accountability partner.

Create a saving journal that all family members can write in to list their accomplishments.

The value of money has the Power to set your family on a positive trajectory. Remember, change in your kids starts with changes with you as the parents!

Have a **beautiful day** on purpose from my heart to yours!

Journal Entry Date: _____

Courageous Action #15

_____

_____

_____

_____

Three Reasons Why This Is Significant for My Life:

Reason One: _____

Reason Two:_____

Reason Three:_____

What Will You Do With This Moment That
Allows It To Be Impactful For You and Others:

_____

_____

_____

_____

_____

What Courageous Conversation Can You Create
From This Action: _____

_____

_____

_____

_____

Week 16 -Going Broke: When a Partner or Your Own Spending is Out of Control

Courageous Conversation: Have you ever wondered how did I or we get here? If so, this entry is for you. It was never your intention to rob Peter to pay Paul; as a matter of fact, you don't even know who Peter and Paul are, yet you've found yourself in a bargaining cycle with these two cats on a monthly basis. Having more month than money was never your intention either, yet month and money seem to be at war with each other in your household on a regular basis. Somehow, you've found yourself in this deep financial well of debt where the bills, bills and more bills have become relentless.

When shopping spirals out of control, and in some cases, becomes an addiction, it can turn into a financial disaster that negatively impacts you, your relationships as well as the entire family.

You may need to have a courageous conversation with yourself and query whether you are in a relationship that is financially abusive or if you and/or your partner have a spending addiction? Either scenario is completely possible for the average person simply trying to maintain.

This entry will discuss why shopping can be so addictive, what the warning signs are, and how to stop the cycle of spending. A Spending Addiction can literally turn your world upside down.

It's important to pay attention to your spending patterns. When you think about how you got here you may find that you have a pattern that lacks discipline and self-control. Constant conflict with your partner over spending too much may be a sign that the spending has moved into an addiction. It's important to note that as overspending moves from dependency to addiction, you need additional support to stop the addiction. You and/or your partner may need therapeutic intervention to assist them in stopping their spending abuse. Often when people have moved into an addiction even if it's a soft addiction like spending it's hard to stop. It seems like a lot of us have difficulty saying no when our friends or even partner's ask us for money. Remember that if they really care about you, they won't try to guilt you if you say no. Sometimes we have to say "no" out of love for ourselves and them versus "yes" out of fear.

Additionally, if someone close to you is always asking you for money, they may have an addiction that you are supporting. It's called enabling and the best thing you can do for them, is to say no. It's hard to say no at first if you are accustomed to always saying yes but you have to practice. The more you practice saying no in a kind and caring way, the more automatic it will become. Feeding others' spending addictions doesn't help them or your relationship.

Keep in mind that all over-spending doesn't lead to a spending addiction. The indicator of a spending addiction is to continue on-going unnecessary spending despite the lack of financial resources and continued negative consequences. Many folks who move into a spending addiction are trying to fill an internal void through this external method of unnecessary spending. Some signs related to spending addiction are as follows:

- When one gets a physiological or emotional rush during and after spending spree. Pay attention to your physiological responses when you or your partner are shopping.
- If you or your partner experience a physiological high that decreases once you have spent all your money this could be a sign that your spending is out of control.
- Spending your mortgage or rent money could land your relationship in divorce court if you don't get help. If both you and your partner have embarked on a co-dependent spending addiction then it will be very difficult for you to help each other kick the habit.

If one partner wants help to arrest the addiction and the other is not be ready to stop spending this could be detrimental to the relationship. In this case, the couple may need external support to address the core issues contributing to the spending abuse.

Call to Action: Make a decision to turn the corner and get help as hard as it may be. Think about which loss is harder; the temporary loss of your ability to spend unconditionally or the loss of your life and your relationship. At some point, your bottom related to loss may be an indicator that you need to get serious about recovery. Recovering from soft addictions like spending are really hard because it's not illegal to overspend and you can't get away from spending so you really have to learn the art of discipline. Make the decision to live a more disciplined life which can ultimately lead to more financial freedom for you and your family.

Have a **beautiful day** on purpose from my heart to yours!

Journal Entry Date: _____

Courageous Action #16

_____

_____

_____

_____

Three Reasons Why This Is Significant for My Life:
Reason One: _____
Reason Two:_____
Reason Three:_____

What Will You Do With This Moment That
Allows It To Be Impactful For You and Others:

_____

_____

_____

_____

_____

What Courageous Conversation Can You Create
From This Action: _____

_____

_____

_____

_____

Week 17-Learning to Combine your Finances as a Healthy Couple

Courageous Conversation: Why do couples fight most over finances? Often times, it's related to trust issues…can I really trust that you will do the right thing so that our family will have financial security?

Money is one of the leading causes of Divorce. But it's not simply money by itself; it's the mismanagement, misunderstanding and often lack of money that are the true culprits leading to the demise of many relationships. Money has the ability to become a vehicle for healthy living but it only works in a relationship if the two parties are on the same page regarding how to manage money.

Have a courageous conversation about your financial patterns of behavior from spending to saving. Come up with a plan to implement both perspectives regarding money into the relationship. If you and your partner land on opposite ends of the spectrum, try to embrace what you both bring to the table that helps you to grow and stretch.

Embrace your differences and similarities. Make them work for you as a couple versus against you as a couple. If you find it difficult to communicate about your finances consider a financial planner/adviser. Also, pay attention to how you have discussed finances for your wedding with your partner or even in your own personal life as a single person. Pay attention to what was modeled in your family; it may help to inform you about your financial patterns as a couple. This will give you a good sense for what you need to work on as a couple. If you don't see eye to eye regarding your finances try to think about the model that you've had versus your partner; it may help you to understand why your ideologies are so different. If you are in agreement about your financial spending as a couple then identify common themes and behaviors that work so that you can repeat this cycle. Remember; our history is meant to inform us not to define us. Determine if you want a similar kind of financial relationship as your parents or do you want something slightly or completely different.

Third parties can help us to get on track if we are open to accepting help from a therapist, coach or mentor. This is a great way to predict your financial future and stay on course as a couple. Remember that you can find some common ground with regards to your finances but you have to work on it. Common ground regarding your finances may require time, professional insight and a willingness to step outside of your comfort zone. Agreeing financially takes time and a better understanding of your relational goals as a couple to make it work. Celebrate your wins as you grow while continuing to identify financial growth areas to work on as a couple. These points of reference are key to achieving your financial wellness both individually and collectively.

__Call to Action__: Make sure you acknowledge each other's contributions in the marriage or relationship in order to balance the ledger regardless of who makes more money.

Remember that money is a powerful resource in a relationship and should not be used as a weapon against the other person. Don't allow money to dictate the power in the relationship. There are many more contributions that balance the ledger besides money. Identify all contributions in your relationship so that all parties feel a sense of reciprocity. Then determine how you will value, manage and utilize your collective resource, (i.e. money) to the benefit of your relationship.

Have a **beautiful day** on purpose from my heart to yours!

Journal Entry Date: _____

Courageous Action #17

_____

_____

_____

_____

Three Reasons Why This Is Significant for My Life:

Reason One: _____

Reason Two:_____

Reason Three:_____

What Will You Do With This Moment That
Allows It To Be Impactful For You and Others:

_____

_____

_____

_____

_____

What Courageous Conversation Can You Create
From This Action: _____

_____

_____

_____

_____

The Cost of Love: & Sex

Here we explore the **Role of Sex,** Intimacy & Vulnerability in Relationships.

In order to have true Intimacy (i.e. In-To-Me-See), both parties must be willing to take a risk to be vulnerable. If either party is unwilling or unable, the path to true and authentic intimacy will be thwarted. Sex can be a major barrier to intimacy when a couple engages in this most important act of intimacy too soon or when the couple has unresolved issues of trust that prevent the two from engaging in acts of sexual satisfaction and mutual sensual affection and affirmation towards each other.

Here we explore:

- How to recharge your relationship battery
- How to sustain, maintain, remain, gain in your relationship
- How to survive an affair and still thrive
- Learning the Art of a healthy sex life in the midst of challenges
- How to stay connected with role changes in relationships

Week 18- Recharge Your Relationship Battery

Courageous Conversation: Have you ever considered that we charge up everything in our lives; cell phones, computers, iPad, cars, you name it, and we charge it. Why don't we give the same consideration to our relationships? They certainly run out of steam and get tired just like anything else.

Relationships are not that different; they require the same amount, if not more care, consideration and attention. The difference between people and things is that we cannot always detect when a relationship battery is low. In this entry, learn how to spot some of the signs that the indicator light in your relationship is on low and in danger of burning out. Then develop ways to recharge your battery and reignite your relationship.

Boredom is one of the first signs of a relationship losing steam. Don't have unrealistic expectations that your relationship won't lose luster at times. Sometimes, unwarranted *aggravation* with a spouse can be about boredom but most times it's about something deeper. Dig deep to see what the root is versus assessing the cause too fast; it could be that the irritation is more about the person who is bored versus the spouse and/or friend.

Neglect can also be a key factor in the relationship losing its zeal. The things each party did in the dating process must continue throughout the duration of the relationship. All relationships have both negative and positive aspects, but you may be losing interest if you're only focused on the negative aspects.

Poor Communication can be lethal to a relationship. Often times our relationships suffer because we focus more on what we don't have versus what we do have. Recharging your relationship battery has to do with establishing healthy communication about your relationship. Don't be afraid to share your concerns in a healthy way with your partner. Holding onto small irritations can build up resentment and diminish healthy energy in your relationship.

Lack of Investment on one side or the other can change our perspective on how we view our relationship. Focus, not on what you don't like but what you do like in your partner. For example, if you are continually finding your partner unattractive versus when you thought that they were the most attractive person on the planet, then it's time to re-evaluate the root of the problem. It's not that they just suddenly became unattractive, it's more about the underlining factors that are contributing to how you now see them. You may need to work on gaining a clearer perspective by spending time re-investing in the relationship.

Re-Investment - All is not lost; ask yourself what would it take to begin reinvesting in your relationship. Begin re-engaging in the conversation and make a commitment to collectively start doing things you use to do with and for your partner. Sparks can get ignited simply by showing interest and effort through a little TLC. Just in case you haven't tried to show your partner a little tender, love and care in quite some time, think about how it might feel with that same level of attention and affection. While there are no guarantees, when you both simultaneously make a commitment to recharge your batteries, there is a high probability that sparks begin to fly.

Call to Action: Start focusing on what connects you to your partner and try to re-capture those moments in the present. Figure out your partners love languages and work on offering them as a gift on a regular basis. You may be surprised at what you get back when you invest a little more energy in your relationship, hence recharging your Relationship Battery.

Have a **beautiful day** on purpose from my heart to yours!

Journal Entry Date: _____

Courageous Action #18

_____

_____

_____

_____

Three Reasons Why This Is Significant for My Life:
Reason One: _____
Reason Two:_____
Reason Three:_____

What Will You Do With This Moment That
Allows It To Be Impactful For You and Others:

_____

_____

_____

_____

_____

What Courageous Conversation Can You Create
From This Action: _____

_____

_____

_____

_____

Week 19- Sustaining, Maintaining, Remaining & Gaining in Your Relationship

Courageous Conversation: Why do some couples only celebrate their relationship once a year on Valentine's or Sweetest Day? Is that really satisfactory for a long-term relationship? Would you only want to get paid for a job you do every day, once a year? Probably not; here's how to have the relationship you want, desire and deserve. If you are not yet in a relationship then these tips are meant to help you in the future when you are in a relationship.

Sustain: If you do celebrate your love on Valentine's or Sweetest Day that's fine, but let's use this day as a barometer for how you will honor your relationship while showing love, like, affirmation, adoration, acceptance and appreciation to your partner daily. Start with making sure your words line up with your actions. In other words, ask yourself the question; does the audio match the video? Remember, what you feed and water lives and what you starve dies. You wouldn't expect for those beautiful flowers in your garden to live and spread their brilliant colors if you never watered them, would you? I didn't think so, so don't expect your relationship to thrive if you don't nurture it.

Plan to have a date night or day at least once a month or more even if you have to date indoors. Get creative if the weather doesn't permit you going outdoors. Think about ways to please your partner and then verbalize your desire first. Keep in mind that it takes five affirming gestures to negate one negative gesture or comment. Thus, if you're constantly putting your partner down or making unsettling comments, you will always be operating from a deficit. Focus on the positive aspects of the relationship versus the negative. You have time to work on the negative aspects of the relationship if both parties are willing participants. Remind yourself that "good-will" goes a long way for the health and wellbeing of your relationship.

Maintain: Continue to focus on what you do have with your partner versus what you don't have. Commit to understanding each other differently and more impactfully. When you know and understand each other better, you will tend to work harder to compromise and do better. Try focusing on "knowing" each other versus constantly "no-ing" each other. Work on forgiveness of your faults and mistakes. Forgiveness is a powerful gift to offer your relationship. Be willing to work at creating a more honest, open and reciprocal relationship with healthy communication, commitment and compromise which will lead to a greater connection.

Remain: Being steadfast and unmovable means that you protect the relationship you believe is sacred even in the midst of challenges. This requires both parties to commit to sticking and staying even when it's hard. Remaining even when things are not quite turning out to be what you signed up for can be difficult. Remember, storms do end and challenges don't last forever. That said, if you both are willing to roll up your sleeves and put the work in by developing the tools, skills, and strategies to not just survive but thrive, you may be glad you remained.

Gain: Remember that developing good communication is hard work. Start with making sure every message sent is the same message received. Focus on listening more than talking. Try to understand your partner because healthy understanding can lead to dissolving unresolved issues. Make sure you have a "team" approach allowing you both to work towards your relationship goals and aspirations together. These strategies will help you to level-up your relationship. As you gain a deeper connection, you will enhance your capacity to grow closer while standing the inevitable test of time.

Call to Action: Here are 7 steps to keep your relationship moving once you've jump started it!

(1) Keep it fresh, try new and exciting things. (2) Make sure you schedule in date nights or date days. (3) Don't lose focus on what matters most. (4) Remember why you fell in love initially and tell your partner regularly. (5) If you have a spiritual foundation pray and/or meditate together daily. (6) Use technology to say I love you to your partner. (7) Feed each other love languages daily.

Have a **beautiful day** on purpose from my heart to yours!

Journal Entry Date: _____

Courageous Action #19

_____

_____

_____

_____

Three Reasons Why This Is Significant for My Life:

Reason One: _____

Reason Two:_____

Reason Three:_____

What Will You Do With This Moment That
Allows It To Be Impactful For You and Others:

_____

_____

_____

_____

_____

What Courageous Conversation Can You Create
From This Action: _____

_____

_____

_____

_____

Week 20- How to Survive an Affair (& Thrive)

Courageous Conversation: Learning of an extra marital affair can spell the end of your marriage or relationship, but it doesn't have to. Many people think that an affair is always the ultimate deal breaker, but what if it's not? What if there was a way to save your relationship and possibly create a better and more satisfying relationship then you had before the affair? Would you be willing to consider this possibility?

Discovering how to heal from the pain, and recover from heartbreak is not an easy proposition. Surviving an affair absolutely requires forgiveness. Whether you reconcile or not, forgiveness liberates you from the toxic emotions related to the violation. It's not whether you will make it through; it's how you will grow through this journey together as a couple or separately as an individual. Once everything is on the table, you may find you can rebuild something very special. Don't expect there to be no conflict. The pain of an affair will take time to heal, so be patient. Manage your information with family and friends. Sharing too much information may not be good for the relationship if you're trying to heal as a couple.

Many folks think they can never make it through an affair, but it's just because you haven't been tested in this way. Don't let your friends tell you what to do in this situation. They may say you should leave the relationship but they could be the very ones that might stay and try to work it out if it happened to them. Your decision to stay or leave should be solely based on your own discernment. However, getting to the point where you're clear about your decision may take some time.

Be patient with yourself and try not to make a hasty decision. Try to consider all related factors before you leap one way or the other. While no one can argue that their partner made them cheat, there are factors related to infidelity. These factors are important to talk about in order to address the root versus just the symptoms. Some things to consider if you are trying to grow through the pain of infidelity are as follows:

- It takes time
- Recovery and rebuilding trust never happens' overnight
- Don't blame yourself but do evaluate what you think happened on both sides
- Don't shy away from talking about your feelings related to the infraction
- If your partner cheated, they have to be willing to acknowledge the pain they caused you, listen and respond to concerns of mistrust in order for there to be any chance of reconciliation
- Couple and/or Individual Therapy is often a must to salvage your relationship after an affair

- Know that certain things may trigger bad feelings even if you feel that you have gotten past it
- Remember, those feelings will decrease over time but may never fully go away
- Both parties should be away of potential triggers and discuss ways to manage them
- Try to focus on other positive aspects of the relationship if you can
- Obsessing on the violation won't help to rebuild trust
- Rebuilding trust requires continual work toward honesty and integrity

Honor your emotions, but remember that forgiveness is available to all of us. Forgiving yourself as well as your partner may be your greatest gift to you and possibly your relationship. Residual effects of the traumatic infraction may occur but this doesn't mean the relationship can't be salvaged. Renewal and restoration are available to you but will require hard work from both parties in order to grow through this particular storm. That said, healing from infidelity is possible, but it will require hope, forgiveness and the right tools to develop a greater and healthier relationship on the other side of the pain.

Call to Action: Make sure you have a support system to assist you during this time. A trusted confidant, spiritual advisor or therapist can be helpful. Asking for help can be a valuable part of the healing process. At some point you will have to stop looking back and start looking forward. It will take time to rebuild trust but you have to want to work at it; if not, it won't work.

If you have children, try not to triangulate them by sharing private information with them about the affair. This will only deposit trust issues into them that will impact their relationships as adults. Get therapeutic support if you need it. It takes true strength not weakness to seek help.

Have a **beautiful day** on purpose from my heart to yours!

Journal Entry Date: _____
Courageous Action #20

_____

_____

_____

_____

Three Reasons Why This Is Significant for My Life:
Reason One: _____

Reason Two:_____

Reason Three:_____

What Will You Do With This Moment That
Allows It To Be Impactful For You and Others:

_____

_____

_____

_____

_____

What Courageous Conversation Can You Create
From This Action: _____

_____

_____

_____

_____

Week 21- Learning the Art of a Healthy Sex Life in Your Relationship in the Midst of Challenges

Courageous Conversation: Are you wondering how to spice up your love life in the bedroom even when life is challenging? If so, perhaps we can start by not assuming that your sex life only needs to occur in the bedroom. Novel idea; right?

Well, part of maintaining and sustaining a healthy sex life is collectively thinking outside the box. When couples get stuck in a sex life routine that they dread where neither party is having healthy and satisfying sex regularly, this can be the beginning of the decline.

After over 20 years as a relationship therapist, I have had hundreds of couples tell me that their sex life was amazing early on in their relationship and when I ask them where things went downhill, most of them say that they started having kids, or they became exhausted due to responsibilities and demands, or that the stressors of life just got the best of them. Usually, neither partner is sure of the exact event or time that their sex life went down the toilet, but they can give voice to how it feels to be so disconnected from such a vital part of their intimate relationship. While these situations are more common than not, there is hope for revitalizing of your sex life even in the midst of challenges. Here are 15 tips to help you re-ignite the spark in your sex life and recapture the vitality in your intimate love life:

- Get out of your head and into your heart
- Set the atmosphere with candles, music and sensual aromas
- Be intentional about re-connecting sexually
- Where sexy or enticing clothing that your partner enjoys viewing
- Step outside of your comfort zone and take risks to be more sensual (words and actions)
- Change locations to create a more exciting sexual experience
- Don't be afraid to verbalize your thoughts about sex as a prelude to the main act
- Try to compartmentalize the stressors and engage in the moment of connection through mindfulness and staying present
- Utilize visual imagery to enhance the sexual connection with your partner
- Remember your initial sexual engagements and what those encounters felt like (share with your partner to recapture those feelings)
- Start intimately connecting with your partner through text /notes during the day
- Protect date night/days as your sacred time
- Fulfill your partner's Love Languages often
- Write an old fashion love letter to your partner and request one back in return
- Create a love journal to share intimate thoughts with each other

---

Call to Action: *Envision what you want, desire and deserve in your sexual relationship. List three ways you distract from what you say you want in a satisfying sexual relationship. Then list three things you can do to improve the sexual intimacy in your relationship. Make a commitment to have a conversation with your partner about the things you both can do to improve your sex life.*

Have a **beautiful day** on purpose from my heart to yours!

Journal Entry Date: _____

Courageous Action #21

_____

_____

_____

_____

Three Reasons Why This Is Significant for My Life:
Reason One: _____
Reason Two:_____
Reason Three:_____

What Will You Do With This Moment That
Allows It To Be Impactful For You and Others:

_____

_____

_____

_____

_____

What Courageous Conversation Can You Create
From This Action: _____

_____

_____

_____

_____

Week 22- Staying Connected When Roles Change in Your Relationship

Courageous Conversation: Have you ever considered the fact that most of us don't like the C word; CHANGE. Yet, in order to be healthy, we all must learn to adapt to change, especially in our relationships.

Changing roles in our relationships can sometimes be overwhelming and difficult. So, how do we talk with our partners about the necessity of change and how to be in healthier relationships when roles have to change due to new jobs, babies, lost jobs, illness, life cycle stages etc. There is an ART to it and you will definitely need to level-up your communication skills.

First, we must accept the fact that there will be times in our lives when we must all learn how to adapt to new norms. These new norms may impose roles changes in our relationships that we did not anticipate. Acceptance is the first step in the process of change. Acceptance doesn't mean that you agree with the change or that you even like the change, it simply means that you are in a better mental space where you accept the fact that change is happening. If we don't accept change, we will continue to bump up against resistance which will ultimately lead to more conflict and disconnection.

Remember that most traditional & non-traditional roles are informally assigned. When there is no formal agreement regarding initial roles or role changes, this can cause relational conflict. Non-verbal agreements about shared responsibilities can create conflict and resentment when there is poor or no communication about those roles.

Much of what we expect as adults has to do with what roles we saw our parents participate in growing up. Those expectations can create conflict if they are very different from what our partners saw growing up. Make sure you talk about these expected roles early in the relationship as well as when the roles change. Often, we as humans identify ourselves through the roles we take on or are assigned. When those stereotypes shift, we can be disappointed which may contribute to relational conflict.

If your roles have changed don't be afraid to talk about your feelings related to those changes. Even though the role changes may be necessary, they still may trigger uncomfortable feelings that can be projected negatively onto your partner or projected from your partner onto yourself.

Expect that your relationship will change due to role changes. Normalize the changes and work towards adapting new norms. Re-evaluate old expectations and work on co-creating new ones. Remember, sometime change is a temporary inconvenience for long-term gain. Adapting and accepting the necessary role changes in your relationship may help to create a closer and more intimate relationship over.

Call to Action: Write a list of the different types of roles you have taken on in your relationship(s) and why. Then check off if it feels congruent & equitable for the relationship. Have a courageous conversation about the roles and how they feel at this stage in the relationship. Make a decision to address the specific roles and any changes that may be needed to adapt to new norms in the relationship. Work towards establishing a new mindset about the importance of your roles and how they contribute to the overall wellbeing of your family and relationship.

Seeking couple therapy or counseling from a spiritual advisor can be helpful to assist in defusing resentment while learning to adapt to the changes in roles.

Have a **beautiful day** on purpose from my heart to yours!

Journal Entry Date: _____

Courageous Action #22

_____

_____

_____

_____

Three Reasons Why This Is Significant for My Life:

Reason One: _____

Reason Two:_____

Reason Three:_____

What Will You Do With This Moment That
Allows It To Be Impactful For You and Others:

_____

_____

_____

_____

_____

What Courageous Conversation Can You Create
From This Action: _____

_____

_____

_____

_____

The Cost of Love: & Kids

Here we explore the **Role of Kids** in Relationships. Challenges around kids, parenting styles, blended families etc. can be significant contributing factors that can make or break a relationship.

In this section we will discuss:

- How to baby proof your relationship
- How to reconnect with your kids without losing yourself in the process
- How to sustain your relationship when your kids are in trouble
- How to thrive in your blended family system versus just surviving

Week 23- Baby Proof Your Relationship

Courageous Conversation: It's an interesting phenomenon when a new baby comes into a system. The entire atmosphere shifts like titanic plates underneath the ground and we need to make adjustments to our old way of thinking and doing. That said, your relationships are important to maintain and there is a delicate balance regarding how you care for that new bundle of joy that's requiring enormous energy and how your care for yourself and your relationships.

Whether you're becoming first time parents, expanding your family with a new baby or transitioning into grand parenthood; learning ways to maintain your healthy relationship(s) is important while you're adjusting to your new norm.

If you are anxious about becoming a new parent and its impact on your relationship, remember fear can paralyze you or it can elevate you. Use your fear as a warning sign to let you know that something powerful and great is happening by bringing life into the world. You have gifts inside you that can make you a great parent but you have to tap into them.

Here are the 5 steps that will help you to adapt to your new parenting role:

- Anticipate the change
- Talk about the change
- Prepare for the change
- Embrace & Accept the change
- Support each other as change happens

Be willing to ask for help and partner with other parents, grandparents, aunties, uncles and friends who can support you.

Unspoken expectations about parental responsibilities can be dangerous to the relationship. Make clear parental responsibility agreements and list them in a common area so that all are on the same page. Because running a household requires completion of many ongoing tasks; couples & families have to really work hard together. Revisit and re-discuss your household distribution of labor agreements monthly to weigh in on how it's working out. If the agreement isn't working or circumstances have changed then talk about changing the agreement to better fit the adaptation of your lifestyle.

Money talks can be hard but necessary. Commit to having honest ongoing talks about your finances and how you as a couple must adapt to growing your family. Accepting changes in how you spend money and what you spend your money on will be key in adapting to your expanding family.

Kids are very adaptable but require predictability, consistency, structure & information. Remember, they may have anxiety about how things will be different once the new baby comes and how their roles will change. Being positive and engaging them in healthy conversation about what to expect can provide just the support they need to adapt.

The great thing about **grandparenthood** is that you don't have to do all the heavy lifting. Think about ways that you can support your child by grand parenting your grandchild(ren) without having a full-time parenting job. Understanding your role as the grandparent is key. While it's a very powerful and necessary role, you must know your limits and try not to cross boundaries into the parenting lane. Making sure you establish clear boundaries as the grandparent can be a healthy position for everyone involved.

Call to Action: Focus on maintaining quality time versus quantity time. Find creative ways to connect even if it's through social media. Try to maintain date night even if you have to barter with other parents by watching their kids once a month & visa versa.

Have a **beautiful day** on purpose from my heart to yours!

Journal Entry Date: _____

Courageous Action #23

_____

_____

_____

_____

Three Reasons Why This Is Significant for My Life:

Reason One: _____

Reason Two:_____

Reason Three:_____

What Will You Do With This Moment That
Allows It To Be Impactful For You and Others:

_____

_____

_____

_____

_____

What Courageous Conversation Can You Create
From This Action: _____

_____

_____

_____

_____

Week 24-Reconnect with Your Kids & Without Losing Yourself

Courageous Conversation: You don't have to sacrifice your entire life as a parent in order to effectively raise your children and launch them into adulthood. However, some parents believe that their life is over once they give birth to these bundles of joy and usher them into the world. Not so……

Ask any parent how life is going, and I guarantee the number one word you'll hear is BUSY. Most parents of children in their formative years are all racing around, tending to jobs, kids' homework, activities and trying to squeeze in a little quality time for themselves and their relationships to the best of their abilities. It's easy to get caught up in the day-to-day grind and feel like there's never any time for more meaningful connections. If this sounds like your life, don't be discouraged. There are some easy ways to reconnect with your children without losing the connection with yourself or your spouse.

Look in the mirror and tell yourself, you matter, you are important and you are worthy of being cared for. If you don't prioritize you, no one else will. Remember, a heathier you is a healthier parent. The four-letter word for LOVE when it comes to children is TIME. That said, there are many things that you can do as a parent that don't require enormous amounts of time while enjoying quality time versus quantity time with your kids. We call this double dipping because you might be participating in these activities already but by being more intentional, it allows you to focus on maintaining the connection rather than just participating in a ritual or routine. Here are 7 areas you can cultivate that help you to reconnect with your kids without losing yourself in the process.

- Turn the gadgets off on the car ride to school and talk about the intentions for the day
- Text your kids a positive affirmation for the day
- Make sure to connect over dinner time versus eating at separate times, in separate places
- Choose one activity a month that you do together; this sets the expectation of something to work towards but does not overwhelm the system
- Create a village that can support you and your kids
- Attend your selected faith-based organization together if you worship somewhere as a family
- Integrate prayer and/or meditation as part of bedtime or meal time

*Call to Action: Meanwhile, don't forget to put your **Oxygen Mask** on first and engage in radical self-care. Make a list of 5 things that you can do for yourself and then be intentional about doing at least one of these things once a week. This will allow you to prioritize yourself through restoration, recalibration and rejuvenation. By taking care of you, you then offer the overflow of yourself to your children as well as your partner versus the residual and depleted part of yourself.*

Have a **beautiful day** on purpose from my heart to yours!

Journal Entry Date: _____

Courageous Action #24

_____

_____

_____

_____

Three Reasons Why This Is Significant for My Life:

Reason One: _____

Reason Two:_____

Reason Three:_____

What Will You Do With This Moment That
Allows It To Be Impactful For You and Others:

_____

_____

_____

_____

_____

What Courageous Conversation Can You Create
From This Action: _____

_____

_____

_____

_____

Week 25-Sustaining Your Relationship When Your Kids are in Trouble

Courageous Conversation: Sometimes we feel like we have to put our relationships on hold when our kids are struggling. Is there a right or wrong answer to this? It's complicated...

The truth is, most of us experience struggles as we journey through life. Just because the person struggling is your child, doesn't mean that they shouldn't have some challenges or that you have to put your entire life on hold. It depends on the nature of the challenges. Clearly, there is a big difference between your child having cancer versus your child having a teenage breakup. Some challenges have the potential to build resilience, strength and develop coping mechanisms to help us grow through future tough times. Other challenges may require more of us as parents to help our children through a difficult terrain.

That said, every relationship in our lives – friendships, family, romantic and professional – can potentially be destroyed by conflict and an inability to manage this conflict effectively. When our kids have problems, this can put an enormous strain on our relationships. If you're trying to manage a relationship while simultaneously trying to help your kids through a tough time, this entry is for you.

Learn how to deal with conflict in your relationship when your kids are in trouble.

Remember, every family experiences conflict with the natural development of children. Some problems are mild, some moderate and some severe. The goal is not to let the conflict divide you. Each parent has a different way of dealing with their child's issues. Remember, it's not right or wrong, just different. If you feel that your child is manipulating you and your partner to purposely cause conflict then talk to your partner about how to handle them together. Children will split if you let them; so, don't let them!

Sometimes step children or even biological children will attempt to create conflict to instigate a break-up or discourse. Keep the lines of communication open so that they are not successful. Many couples argue more if they allow the child(ren) to manipulate the relationship. Remember who is in charge of the system and don't stop talking with each other. Giving up on talking about it is the worst thing you can do.

Additionally, conflict can occur with the grandparents as well as other family members if they interfere with what the parents' decision is for their kids who are in trouble. Make sure that you and your partner are in agreement before you allow the grandparents or other family members intervene. Everyone has a role and it does take a village, but there must be alignment with the parents first, in order to keep the relationship intact while supporting the child(ren). Keeping the lines of communication open is key throughout the ups and downs of parenting. This will help you to keep your parenting boundaries intact.

Call to Action: *Communications is key when there is conflict over kids. To dissolve guilt or blame shifting behavior, having couple and family meetings are essential to everyone getting on the same page. There are no guarantees with parenting. Bad things happen to all of us. Exhale, use your support system and try not to internalize any of it. Normalize your kids' problems. Don't forget; all people have problems, even little people. Try to reduce your conflict by recalling the problems you had growing up and how you made it through. Share those with your kid(s) and partner. Seek additional support if you need it through spiritual counseling or couple & family therapy.*

Have a **beautiful day** on purpose from my heart to yours!

Journal Entry Date: _____

Courageous Action #25

_____

_____

_____

_____

Three Reasons Why This Is Significant for My Life:
Reason One: _____
Reason Two:_____
Reason Three:_____

What Will You Do With This Moment That
Allows It To Be Impactful For You and Others:

_____

_____

_____

_____

_____

What Courageous Conversation Can You Create
From This Action: _____

_____

_____

_____

_____

Week 26 -Thriving in Your Blended Family

Courageous Conversation: If you think it's easy combining two families into one, think again. Many have tried and many have failed. It's important to think about all the factors that can make or break you as a family system. Most people who have done it successfully will tell you that it may go down in history as one of the hardest things that they've ever done. With that being said, it is not impossible to have an intact and successful blended family. But in order to accomplish this, it takes WORK!

According to the American Academy of Matrimonial Lawyer (AAML), at least 66% of second marriages fail. The reasons? People don't deal with and heal personal issues that played a role in the demise of their first marriage or relationship before entering into another relationship or remarrying. Additionally, the pressure of raising bonus children along with biological children, not to mention baby momma or poppa drama often causes more conflict then the marriage can handle.

If this reminds you of your blended family, this entry is for you. Let's talk about some healthy ways you can blend your new family successfully.

- Throw your pride in the toilet. You can either be prideful and make excuses and or be humble and make adjustments. Either way, your children will experience the fallout or residual effect of your choices.

- Focus on your children's health and wellbeing. Consider that your children didn't ask to be a part of a blended family yet, they may suffer the consequences of circumstances that they didn't create.
- Change your expectations and focus on what you can control versus what you can't control.
- Be patient with the process. Growth and healing take time. Give yourself time to heal while focusing on the end game. Creating a healthy blended family is more like a marathon than a sprint.
- Communicate your intentions to your children and reframe from triangulating them into any conflict between you or their parents. They don't deserve to suffer in the middle of your painful relationship.
- Reframe from talking about your ex-partner to your children or in the presence of your children.
- Don't make your child(ren) your confidant with respect to any past family drama. They are not you or your ex-partner's friends and should not be thrust into inappropriate peer like relationships with adults due to unresolved issues.

Call to Action: Seek couple, family and/or individual therapy for yourself and your family if any of you are struggling to adjust to your new norm as a blended family. Adapting to a Blended family dynamic is difficult so remind yourself that it's okay to ask for help on your journey to healing.

Have monthly family meetings to discuss how everyone is adjusting to your new norm. Share what's working and what's not working so that everyone has a voice!

Start spending quality time together as a family. Take turns with each person choosing a monthly activity. By do this you will begin to establish new family norms and rituals leading to family connection.

Have a **beautiful day** on purpose from my heart to yours!

Journal Entry Date: _____

Courageous Action #26

_____

_____

_____

_____

Three Reasons Why This Is Significant for My Life:

Reason One: _____

Reason Two:_____

Reason Three:_____

What Will You Do With This Moment That
Allows It To Be Impactful For You and Others:

_____

_____

_____

_____

_____

What Courageous Conversation Can You Create
From This Action: _____

_____

_____

_____

_____

Week 27- Helping Your Anxious Kids Overcome Their Fears & Phobias

Courageous Conversation: Have you ever wondered if your child's fears are valid or simply a figment of their imagination? Well, sometimes the answer is yes and yes. It's very possible that they may have real fears and/or phobias and that they could be an internal part of their imagination.

Things that go bump in the night, a teacher's harsh rebuke or crying out for a parent who is not there. What do they all have in common? Plenty, they're all typical childhood anxieties and fears.

Nothing to worry too much about, but try telling that to your child is another story. As a parent, you can make a big difference in how well your child handles common worries like these. This entry offers ways that can help you and your child manage those fears with a greater level of understanding. Children will show you better than they can tell you about their fears. Here are 10 areas to address when dealing with your children's fears:

- Pay attention to warning signs that are demonstrated through your child's behavior.
- Don't ignore your child's complaints; they may be the key to helping them resolve their fears.
- Try not to project your fears onto your children. Often, we model as adults the fears our children will acquire.

- Have them write down or draw how their fears make them feel. This will help you understand how to help them.
- Don't be afraid to have a healthy conversation with your child about their fears. Often negative experiences will manifest themselves in phobias that mask as fears.
- Often a book or a good movie that represents a similar situation can be a great ice breaker and help you to start the conversation with them about their fears.
- Being stuck or paralyzed is a prevalent symptom related to certain fears. Try to normalize it and create steps to help your child to grow through it. This can be very helpful to arresting the fear itself.
- Recognize that fears can be transgenerational patterns that plague the whole family if gone unaddressed.
- Partner with your child or children to address all of their fears as a family affair so they feel supported.
- Don't be afraid to seek additional therapeutic support to help your child address and resolve their fears.

Call to Action: If the fears seem less pronounced, create a safe space for you and your child to talk about them in order to ease their concerns. Providing a safe and secure environment will go a long way in comforting your child and easing your worry as a parent.

If the fears seem more profound, select a good child and family therapist to assist your child with these childhood fears. If left unaddressed, these fears have the potential to develop into more serious phobias that can negatively impact your child's success. There is help...you just have to be willing to seek out support.

Have a **beautiful day** on purpose from my heart to yours!

Journal Entry Date: _____

Courageous Action #27

_____

_____

_____

_____

Three Reasons Why This Is Significant for My Life:

Reason One: _____

Reason Two:_____

Reason Three:_____

What Will You Do With This Moment That
Allows It To Be Impactful For You and Others:

_____

_____

_____

_____

_____

What Courageous Conversation Can You Create
From This Action: _____

_____

_____

_____

_____

CHAPTER 3
STAYING HEALTHY IN THE MIDST OF TRANSITIONS

Week 28- Nothing's Constant but Change

Courageous Conversation: Change happens whether we like it or not, the question is will you be ready when change comes knocking at your door?

Most of us are fearful or resistive to change but we must remember that nothing is constant but change. Even though we gravitate to the things, people and experiences that are familiar, it's a wonderful thing to experience the gifts of change. The best way to realize your own resilience and power is to face the transition head on. Remember that for every new phase in life, we will need a new set of skills and resources to help us transition more smoothly. Yet, those new phases are all reminders that we made it through the previous phases. What a blessing!

Make sure to remember what brought you through your past transitions so that you will gain the confidence to know that you have what it takes to grow through the next transition. Additionally, while we are trying to figure it out; God has already worked it out. Our part is to accept and embrace our life cycle transitions in order to go to our next level. Pay attention to the ways you may be engaging in sabotaging behavior out of your fear of change. If you know someone or something is not good for you or to you, yet you can't tolerate what it may feel like to let him, her, them or it go, then you may be sabotaging yourself.

If we don't adapt to change, we will stay stuck in the past unable to experience the present or anticipate the beauty of our future. It's similar to being on a plane that is stuck in a holding pattern, you are unable to experience getting to your destination, yet the previous location is already behind you. At some point we have to land and make a decision to accept the transition so that we can move forward to enjoy the journey.

Call to Action: Remember, we all experience life cycle changes. For example, empty nesters can either focus on the kids being gone or embrace all that their next stage has to offer. A job loss may be devastating, but opens you up to becoming a successful entrepreneur.

If you are resistive to adapting to your new norm begin to journal all the ways your life can be positively transformed as a result of the changes. Then list all the areas in your life that you would like to develop and write down action steps to incorporate those new experiences. Change is happening whether you like it or not, so go with it and see what happens. You might be pleasantly surprised at the version of yourself and the life you are creating if you are open to it.

Have a **beautiful day** on purpose from my heart to yours!

Journal Entry Date: _____

Courageous Action #28

_____

_____

_____

_____

Three Reasons Why This Is Significant for My Life:

Reason One: _____

Reason Two:_____

Reason Three:_____

What Will You Do With This Moment That
Allows It To Be Impactful For You and Others:

_____

_____

_____

_____

_____

What Courageous Conversation Can You Create
From This Action: _____

_____

_____

_____

_____

Week 29- Managing Life's Transitions

Courageous Conversation: Have you ever taken into consideration that people don't plan to fail they fail to plan?

Sometimes we fail to plan because we are too comfortable in our present state and we recognize that if we begin to plan, things will change in ways that we may not be prepared to adapt to.

Begin to think about what you can do to adapt to the change in your life in a healthy way. Sitting with unknowns requires patience and trust in the process. Unknowns are hard to swallow but remember, if nothing changes; nothing changes. Adaptation is a necessary coping skill in this world of constant changes. Never assume that your life and/or relationship will always be the same. Things change for good or bad; better or worse. All of us will find the need to adapt to changes at some point in our lives.

Many relationships have difficulty surviving major changes. Seek additional support in the mists of a major change to help you as an individual or couple to navigate the process of change. Healthy communication is essential to a couple's ability to weather the storm of change. How you as a couple or individual respond to major changes in your relationship may make the difference in your resilience and ability to both survive and thrive.

None of us is able to grow without change and transition. It is the way that we as humans continue to evolve. Change can also be painful to accept when the thing that is changing is not what we want. That said, once we have managed to grow through it, we usually find out how strong we really are and how much better and wiser we are for having the transition.

Call to Action: List all the changes that you have adapted to over the course of your life. Then list next to the changes the coping strategies you developed as a result of your transitions. You may find that you are stronger than you thought you were. Celebrate your strengths and your ability to adapt to good and bad transitions. Your future is depending on it.

Have a **beautiful day** on purpose from my heart to yours!

Journal Entry Date: _____

Courageous Action #29

_____

_____

_____

_____

Three Reasons Why This Is Significant for My Life:

Reason One: _____

Reason Two:_____

Reason Three:_____

What Will You Do With This Moment That
Allows It To Be Impactful For You and Others:

_____

_____

_____

_____

_____

What Courageous Conversation Can You Create
From This Action: _____

_____

_____

_____

_____

Week 30- Adapting to Career Changes, New Roles & its' Impact on Your Relationship

Courageous Conversation: Why do you think that many of us define ourselves by the work that we do? It's a phenomenon that has persisted for hundreds of years. Yet, should we really define ourselves by our vocation? What happens when the thing we chose or that chose us, is no longer a viable option for any number of reasons; do we then cease to be human?

Ask yourself the question; have I been socialized to define myself by the job that I do or the professional career that I've chosen. If so, do I still add value to the world, my family and friends when I am no longer physically, mentally or financially able to do that job or participate in that particular career field.

Because most of us define ourselves by the work that we do, it makes it even more painful when we no longer have the job title to define ourselves by. The truth is, our jobs were never meant to define us in the first place. Our jobs are not who we are as human beings; our jobs represent what we do to make a living and hopefully make a difference. It's been said that we should be careful not to be so busy making a living that we forget to live. Living life like it's golden outside of your work/career life will help you when these inevitable transitions come to pass.

Talking about new expectations is key when you get a new job but it's also equally as important when you lose your job, switch roles or careers or embark on a journey of entrepreneurship. All of these transitions, no matter how you got there require a new level of skill to navigate this unknown territory.

Try to think of job or career change as a temporary situation versus permanent. In essence, it may be a temporary inconvenience that can lead to long term gain. Even if you are promoted, any change will come with an adjustment for yourself as well as those connected to you. If your roles shift in your personal life due to job and/or career changes, talk about why and if you need to revisit certain roles once things change again and how everyone is adapting to their new roles and responsibilities during the transition.

New job responsibilities can be personalized if the couple has lost quantity time together. Especially if the job requires us to spend more time away from home. That's why making quality time so sacred is essential for those times when there won't be much quantity time.

Call to Action: *Set aside time to journal your feelings about your transitions. Write a letter to your partner if you are having a difficult time conveying to them how the new transition regarding work or other changes feel to you. Ask for them to write back so you will have a foundation from which to begin a courageous conversation about the impact of the job or career change. Whatever, you are feeling; be willing to communicate honestly with yourself and your partner. Remember, truth, trust and transparency lead to transformational breakthroughs.*

Have a **beautiful day** on purpose from my heart to yours!

Journal Entry Date: _____

Courageous Action #30

_____

_____

_____

_____

Three Reasons Why This Is Significant for My Life:

Reason One: _____

Reason Two:_____

Reason Three:_____

What Will You Do With This Moment That
Allows It To Be Impactful For You and Others:

_____

_____

_____

_____

_____

What Courageous Conversation Can You Create
From This Action: _____

_____

_____

_____

_____

Week 31- Job Loss: When Bad Things Happen to Good People

Courageous Conversation: If you are struggling with your partner because you or they lost a job, remember, every relationship has its season of struggle.

The journey of unemployment will not last forever. This too shall pass; it's just a matter of time. Faith and patience are two main ingredients to surviving job loss.

While it may be time to tighten your wallet, it's not time to wage war on you partner. Trust that your partner can handle the courageous conversations. Remember, you need to "talk it out" so you don't "act it out" in your relationship. Surviving something difficult like job loss requires determination, lots of communication and prayer. Your relationship can not only survive, but it can thrive if you really want it and are willing to do the work.

You may have to discuss what changes need to be made with your lifestyle in order to weather the job-loss storm. Depression is normal when we go through life's challenges so be patient with the process.

Call to Action: Be willing to ask for help even when you don't want to. Make sure you don't suffer in silence. Talk with your partner about your emotional state. Therapy or spiritual counseling can be a lifeline to your relationship and family during the job loss period. It takes true strength not weakness to seek help. Remember, job loss is a temporary state of being. This particular storm will not last forever. At the end of storms rainbows appear to indicate that the storm is over. Your rainbow is coming, just have faith.

Have a **beautiful day** on purpose from my heart to yours!

Journal Entry Date: _____

Courageous Action #31

_____

_____

_____

_____

Three Reasons Why This Is Significant for My Life:
Reason One: _____

Reason Two:_____

Reason Three:_____

What Will You Do With This Moment That
Allows It To Be Impactful For You and Others:

_____

_____

_____

_____

_____

What Courageous Conversation Can You Create
From This Action: _____

_____

_____

_____

_____

Week 32- Avoiding the Resentment Flu

Courageous Conversation: Do you ever wonder why two people who are experiencing a difficult transition start blaming and shaming each other versus affirming and supporting one another?

Sometimes, we tend to start projecting onto our partners and blame shifting because it's easier to project out than to look within. I like to call these thoughts the "resentment flu". It's like coming down with the flu which is very different from a common cold; it's so hard to recover from and it kind of hits you from the blind side unexpectedly. That said, it's not impossible to recover from the resentment flu.

Overcoming resentment flu must start with understanding the origin of the resentment. In other words, what are you really mad about? We're typically never mad about the surface stuff; resentment always runs deeper. Start by trying to understand the root of the resentment. Then be willing to talk about it in an open and honest way without unfair fighting. The next step is to truly work on the forgiveness process. Ultimately, without forgiveness and the other party acknowledging the injury then the resentment will more than likely continue to grow. Sometimes resentment can outgrow the relationship ultimately leading to the demise of it. This is why it's so important to communicate about relationship injuries, unwanted changes, unexpected transitions etc. before they grow into deep resentment spiraling out of control.

Resentment can build up if a partner believes that their partner is using work, hobbies, organizations, friends or family as an escape from the relationship. Many people don't just have affairs with people; they sometimes have affairs with their jobs, careers, extended family and more, leaving little room to nurture their relationship. Those who fit the characteristics of a workaholic or absentee partner may find themselves being married to work and using their job or extracurricular activities as an excuse to avoid home, kids or their partners.

Focus on quality time versus quantity time. Keep your couple time sacred which will help the both parties feel valued. Try to create balance to the best of your ability. It's so easy to lose balance in a relationship yet it is very hard to get it back. That said, while it's not impossible to get back on track, it will take hard work and commitment. Regaining balance once things have spun out of control is somewhat like putting the town back together once the Tornado is over.

Balance requires that both parties re-focus their energies into the things that matter most. Then they have to make a sincere commitment not to allow lots of very powerful things, events and people move them away from their commitment to stay connected. Sometimes it requires developing the skillful art of saying no and not feeling guilty. Especially if the request is relocating you or your relationship back to that state of chaos and unbalance. Balance can be a moving target which requires us to stay focused on maintaining it once we have it. It will sometimes elude us when unfortunate or unpredictable things happen but we must try to regain it before it spins out of control again. Maintaining a healthy balance in our lives and relationships is essential to healthy living. Without it, our lives become so much more stressful, non-enjoyable and unhealthy physically, mentally, emotionally, relationally and spiritually.

Call to Action: *Re-evaluate your initial commitment to each other monthly. Try to stay focused on "I" statements becoming solution oriented regarding what you can do to stay on target with your commitment to each other.*

Utilize these 5 steps: pause, breath, reflect, identify triggers and then respond with understanding versus anger. This will help to decrease the probability of the Resentment Flu creeping back into your relationship.

Have a **beautiful day** on purpose from my heart to yours!

Journal Entry Date: _____

Courageous Action #32

_____

_____

_____

_____

Three Reasons Why This Is Significant for My Life:
Reason One: _____
Reason Two:_____
Reason Three:_____

What Will You Do With This Moment That
Allows It To Be Impactful For You and Others:

_____

_____

_____

_____

_____

What Courageous Conversation Can You Create
From This Action: _____

_____

_____

_____

_____

Week 33- Rebuilding Your Emotional Strength Muscles

Courageous Conversation: How strong are your emotional muscles? It's easy for our negative emotions to get the best of us leaving us feeling weaker than we ever imagine ourselves to be. The truth is that many of us don't realize that we are stronger than we think. We just have to grow our emotional strength muscles.

Bad things happen to good people and have the potential to disrupt good relationships. The question isn't whether you'll face struggles, but how you'll handle them when they come. When the going gets tough, the tough often gets going. What will it take to preserve and strengthen you as well as your relationship in the long run? Even the healthiest of relationships can be challenged in the aftermath of unexpected trauma, tragedy or loss. To grow through a storm will require more of you than you may imagine. Thus, it's important that you think about how to access the deeper part of you where your emotional strength muscles are. They are inside of you; you just have to tap into them and start using them to help you through this particular storm. Here are a few things that may help you access them:

- Change your perspective.
- Readjust your expectations.
- Be Patient with yourself.
- As opposed to asking why me; challenge yourself to ask, why not me?
- Remember that there are other people in the world that may have worse challenges than you.
- Identify one thing to be grateful for every day.
- Remind yourself that this too shall pass.
- Envision your life on the other side of this challenge.
- Seek therapy or trusted confident to process emotional feelings.

You are stronger than you think but it's not enough for others to believe it. You have to go deeper in your belief in yourself. As you build your inner strength be reminded of how many successful battles you've been in and celebrate the ones you've come through victoriously. This should help you in re-building faith in your emotional strength muscles to see you through.

Call to Action: Make a decision to embark on a journey feeling whatever your emotions are related to the pain. Your emotional strength muscles are inside of you ready and waiting for you to use them. Have a gratitude journal and a process journal. Write your feelings out daily to externalize them. Remember, in order to heal you, have to feel and you can't feel what you don't reveal.

Have a **beautiful day** on purpose from my heart to yours!

Journal Entry Date: _____

Courageous Action #33

_____

_____

_____

_____

Three Reasons Why This Is Significant for My Life:

Reason One: _____

Reason Two:_____

Reason Three:_____

What Will You Do With This Moment That
Allows It To Be Impactful For You and Others:

_____

_____

_____

_____

_____

What Courageous Conversation Can You Create
From This Action: _____

_____

_____

_____

_____

Week 34- Here Comes the Bride: Ready, Set, Go...

Courageous Conversation: Have you ever wondered why so many people who wait a lifetime to say I do, tend to focus more on planning the wedding that will last for a day, but not planning the marriage which is supposed to last a lifetime?

Even with all the memories of that beautiful day, you will still need more then pictures and the top of the frozen wedding cake to be successful. Marriages require work and those who are most successful at it understand this realization. You would never go to a job interview and say; I'm lazy, I'm not a team player, I don't like to communicate and I don't care about getting better but then expect for someone to hire you. Nor would you go to an ATM machine and expect to make a withdrawal from your account when you have deposited nothing in it. A marriage is an entity that you must invest in for the rest of your lives together if you expect reciprocity and a return on your investment. It requires work and lots of adjustments in the transition from singlehood to marriage-hood.

Make a decision to put the work in by communicating regularly with your partner about your marriage. Both parties must be willing to have courageous conversations to celebrate what's going well along with highlighting the things that are not going so well. You both must be willing to course correct quickly when your words, deeds or actions have contributed to hurting the other person. Be willing to evaluate your progress over if you have agreed to honor a request for change. Be intentional about the assets you bring to the marriage and be clear about your wants, desires and needs.

Compromise, communication, commitment and connection are key elements in the health and wellbeing of your marriage. Be open to exploring the levels of satisfaction and/or dissatisfaction in your relationship so that you can enjoy what's working and improve the things that are not quite where you want them to be. No relationship is perfect, but you can enjoy being perfect for each other if you are intentional about staying engaged in the ongoing process of relational growth and development individually and collectively. Being on the same team is key. There is nothing like knowing without a shadow of a doubt your partner who wants you to win in life and that you are both in it to win it. This kind of thinking can result in collective wins for your marriage over the course of your lifetime of love.

Call to Action: Make a list of all the areas that you are excelling in within your relationship and any areas that you feel you still need to work on. Make a commitment to celebrate those areas where you are doing well in and roll up your sleeves get to work on those growth areas that need improvement.

Seek Pre-marital Counseling if you need help communicating about the hot button areas in order to gain clarity, create compromise and find common ground. Then, enjoy the journey into matrimony. It can be a wonderful experience of sharing the rest of your life with someone you love. Oh, enjoy the wedding too!

Have a **beautiful day** on purpose from my heart to yours!

Journal Entry Date: _____

Courageous Action #34

_____

_____

_____

_____

Three Reasons Why This Is Significant for My Life:

Reason One: _____

Reason Two:_____

Reason Three:_____

What Will You Do With This Moment That
Allows It To Be Impactful For You and Others:

_____

_____

_____

_____

_____

What Courageous Conversation Can You Create
From This Action: _____

_____

_____

_____

_____

Week 35- The Ins and Outs of In-Laws

Courageous Conversation: Isn't interesting how in-laws can be a tremendous source of support and closeness or they can also be a major problem in your marital relationship.

If you need help understanding how to deal with your extended family in a healthy way, this entry is for you. Learning to manage the relationships with your in-laws can be challenging yet doable. If you are having difficulty connecting with your in-laws or extended family, talking with your spouse may help you to feel more supported. Remember, true acceptance may not happen right away. All healthy relationships take time to develop so try to be patient. Don't try to force it; allow the process to unfold naturally. Be patient and be yourself; don't pretend to be someone you're not just to please your spouse's family.

Remember how strong those bonds are. Don't get into the weeds with your spouse about your in-laws. Try to be honest without being hurtful or disrespectful. Using "I" statements and sticking to the facts may help your case and enable you to make your point more successfully.

Here are 10 signs that your spouse may be unable to cut the apron strings:

1. Spending excessive time with in-laws versus your new nuclear family.
2. Not being able to establish your own family rules of engagement.
3. Sharing too much personal information about your relationship with spouse.
4. Unable to set appropriate boundaries with the in-laws
5. Allowing in-laws dictate to direction of the relationship and/or marriage.
6. Allowing in-laws to guilt partner into agreeing to do things without the agreement of the other partner.
7. Submitting to requests that go against the relationship agreements.
8. Loaning money without both parties being in agreement.
9. Allowing in-laws to talk poorly about the spouse without addressing negative behavior.
10. Being unwilling to establish new household agreements due to attachments to old family rituals.

Healthy differentiation takes time but is necessary for a new couple to establish their own nuclear unit. We often look subconsciously for someone like our parents. Try to focus on your in-laws' positive attributes that you both have in common. Work on creating new rituals that you both are comfortable with. Agree to maintain one of the old family rituals perhaps with your in-laws and establish one new family ritual perhaps without your in-laws.

If your in-laws offer unsolicited advice when it comes to conducting your relationship or parenting style, evaluate if the advice is helpful or not. Thank them for the suggestion but don't agree to follow it unless you really want to and are in agreement with your spouse. Become comfortable with saying you will think about it but not commit to it. This will give you time to process whether it works for your new family system or not.

If you feel excluded from your spouse's family at times, recognize that inclusion takes time. It may come about way after the marriage. Don't sweat it. Focus on making sure there is inclusion in your relationship with your spouse. When we think of our in-laws, we should be thinking that we are gaining family members, but remember, just like it's taken a lifetime to connect to your family, it will also take some time to connect to your new extended family.

Call to Action: Try to integrate the value systems from both families of origin. Don't assume it has to be only one way. Embrace both sides and decide which values you will integrate and which ones you will toss. Don't let the in-laws guilt you or your partner into submitting to their way.

Make a commitment to co-create your ideal partnership by writing a vision plan for your relationship that incorporates both parties' core values, principles and beliefs. In doing this you can agree on how much input your in-laws will have in your relationship. From this plan work towards creating your relationship mission statement. This will allow you to have healthy relationship with your in-laws and your partner.

Have a **beautiful day** on purpose from my heart to yours!

Journal Entry Date: _____

Courageous Action #35

_____

_____

_____

_____

Three Reasons Why This Is Significant for My Life:

Reason One: _____

Reason Two:_____

Reason Three:_____

What Will You Do With This Moment That
Allows It To Be Impactful For You and Others:

_____

_____

_____

_____

_____

What Courageous Conversation Can You Create
From This Action: _____

_____

_____

_____

_____

Week 36- Becoming Parents

Courageous Conversation: Have you wondered why some people tune into great parents and others are colossal failures at parenting?

Even more interesting is that those parents who are pretty awful at parenting, often think that they're great parents and those who question their parenting skills, often are better parents than they actually realize.

The truth is that some parents should never have signed up for the job. They're not good at it and are unwilling and/or unable to put the work in to become more skilled at it. Many people take parenthood too lightly when in fact, it's one of the most important jobs anyone can ever do in their lifetime. It requires a high skill level and continual on the job training. This is why many people have to level-up their priorities and why many people who embark on this journey of parenting change so drastically once they become parents.

Changes & transitions are inevitable if you are considering becoming a new parent. If you embark on this journey without any expectation of change, you are in for a rude awakening. Not only will your body change, but how you react to things will more than likely change. You are becoming solely responsible for another human being on this planet for at least two decades or more. Thus, the transition of becoming new parents can be daunting. Here are a few things to consider to help you along the way.

-Focus on being healthy physically, mentally and spiritually.

-Make planning a priority.

-Ask for support before and after the baby arrives.

-Be patient with yourself and your partner; it's new terrain that you might not have traveled before.

-Try to create SELFIE Time – Find time to put your oxygen mask on first and give yourself a break.

-Be consistent with date night to nurture your relationship. Make sure you have great baby sitters you trust.

-Consider non-traditional support such as a Duala; this may provide the entire family with the support that is needed.

Call to Action: Keep a parenthood journal and an old school scrapbook. Be intentional about enjoying the journey of parenthood; time flies and before you know it you will be launching those little people who grow up fast off to college to live their best lives. You don't want to miss a minute of it! That said, remember that you are human too. Be honest with yourself when you need breaks and make sure your village is there fill in when you need to re-fuel for the next shift.

Have a **beautiful day** on purpose from my heart to yours!

Journal Entry Date: _____
Courageous Action #36

_____

_____

_____

_____

Three Reasons Why This Is Significant for My Life:
Reason One: _____
Reason Two: _____
Reason Three: _____

What Will You Do With This Moment That
Allows It To Be Impactful For You and Others:

_____

_____

_____

_____

_____

What Courageous Conversation Can You Create
From This Action: _____

_____

_____

_____

_____

Week 37- The Launching Process: Empty Nesters Gone Right

Courageous Conversation: Have you ever wondered why parents spend almost two decades raising children with the hopes of launching them into adulthood successfully and then have difficulty letting go when it's time to let them fly?

If this reminds you of yourself, then this conversation is for you. The launching process can be quite a challenge, whether you're becoming empty nesters or flying the coop yourself, transitions are hard. It appears that birds have figured it out quicker than us humans. They spend weeks preparing their nest for the delivery of their bay birds to hatch, but after they have given them everything they need to survive; they begin to make that cozy nest more uncomfortable by taking the feathers out of the nest. What's left in the nest are prickly branches. The goal is to not allow their baby birds to get too comfortable while preparing them to fly into their independence and self-sufficiency. In order to do this, momma and poppa bird must be willing to let go early enough to ensure that their babies will survive and thrive without them.

Remember that the launching process allows you as a parent renewed freedom if you are receptive to it. A launching process refers to teens moving into adulthood as well as parents launching them from adolescence into adulthood. It also relates to anyone who may be launching into a different phase in their lives; launching into college life, graduate school, the world of work, parenting, retirement etc. No matter what location you are being launched to, when the fear of the unknown attempts to paralyze you, try to think about when you were scared before and how you grew through that experience.

New experiences are always challenging, but if you run away from them, you will never know how it feels to embrace them. When we are fearful of change or hesitant of transitions, it's usually because we doubt our internal power and fear the unknown. We must realize that we already have the power to adapt to any change that reveals itself; our internal power is innate. The next step is to accept that change is inevitable. This will enable us to embrace our ability to launch someone else, like our children or to be launched to the next destination ourselves while enjoying the journey. Launching is a necessary part of growth; without it we stay stuck.

__Call to Action:__ Resist the urge to give away your power by staying stuck in what's familiar. The only true failure is never trying. Take the risk to go to your next level by launching you or your kids. In life, launching one's self or being launched is a necessity not an option. So, what are you waiting for?

Spread your wings and fly!!!

Have a **beautiful day** on purpose from my heart to yours!

Journal Entry Date: _____

Courageous Action #37

_____

_____

_____

_____

Three Reasons Why This Is Significant for My Life:

Reason One: _____

Reason Two:_____

Reason Three:_____

What Will You Do With This Moment That
Allows It To Be Impactful For You and Others:

_____

_____

_____

_____

_____

What Courageous Conversation Can You Create
From This Action: _____

_____

_____

_____

_____

Week 38- When Chronic Illness in the Family Impacts Your Relationship

Courageous Conversation: Life is going along smoothly when all of a sudden you hit a bump in the road. A loved one, spouse, child or other relative has been diagnosed with an illness. How do you cope? What do you do? This is a dilemma that many of us can't escape albeit we might want to desperately avoid the inevitable.

Most relationships are challenged by illness. There is strength in the struggle. Relationships can grow through the struggle but may have to go deeper with their prayer life as well as their spiritual relationship.

Sometimes we have to learn to anticipate the curve balls like illness so that we're not caught off guard and blind-sided. Smooth lines are often few and far between in this obstacle course we call life. When we are faced with illness, we can always draw on having made it through the last illness in the family if you've had one. If you've never tackled major illness in your intimate relationships then you are truly blessed. However, please know that if you live long enough this circumstance will happen in your life sooner or later.

It's best to be prepared by practicing a few things:

- Practice prayer.
- Practice the power of being positive.
- Practice believing in God's provision for whatever you need.
- Practice understanding the purpose of your role so that you can use it during this time.
- Practice asking for help.

Remember, nothing lasts forever. This too shall pass; it's just a matter of time. Faith and patience are two main ingredients in surviving illness. Be patient with yourself and go deeper in your faith. It's not whether you will make it through; it's how you will grow through this journey.

If you have had conflicts with family members like siblings or extended relatives over participation of your loved one's care, this is not the time to wage war on your family. People just become more of who they have always been when issues of money, death and illness hit close to home. Don't have unrealistic expectations. Only focus on what you can do, not what others are or are not doing.

If you have difficulty talking with your partner about your feelings related to their illness or your loved one's illness, trust that your partner can handle these courageous conversations. Taking the risk to share your pain will only deepen your level of intimacy with your partner. Remember, you need to talk it out so you don't act it out in your relationship. Belief in the strength of your relationship will help you to not only survive but even thrive. Surviving a family member's illness requires determination, lots of communication and prayer. Make sure you have multiple support systems to assist you during this difficult time. Your support may come from people you least expect.

Your relationship can not only survive but it can thrive if you really want it. That said, you have to be willing to ask for help even when you don't want to. Resist the urge to not take people up on their offer. You may have to discuss what changes need to be made with your lifestyle in order to weather the storm of illness. Denial won't work; remember the only thing constant is change. Be prepared to make adjustments to your lifestyle and don't feed into others guilt trips.

Depression is normal when we go through life's challenges. Make sure you don't suffer in silence. Talk with your partner or confidant about your emotional state. Good cries are helpful too, as long as you don't stay in an emotionally paralyzing space for ever. God can handle all your emotions and will help you process everything including your anger. Also, therapeutic support can help if you need it.

Call to Action: Therapy or spiritual counseling can be a lifeline to your relationship and family during this period of illness. It takes true strength not weakness to seek help. Remember, you won't be helpful to the person who is ill if you don't take good care of yourself emotionally, mentally, relationally, physically & spiritually. You owe it to yourself to level-up with support to grow you through this difficult time. Make a decision to ask for help and give yourself permission to receive help to strengthen you through this particular journey.

Have a **beautiful day** on purpose from my heart to yours!

Journal Entry Date: _____

Courageous Action #38

_____

_____

_____

_____

Three Reasons Why This Is Significant for My Life:

Reason One: _____

Reason Two:_____

Reason Three:_____

What Will You Do With This Moment That
Allows It To Be Impactful For You and Others:

_____

_____

_____

_____

_____

What Courageous Conversation Can You Create
From This Action: _____

_____

_____

_____

_____

Week 39- Losing a Loved One: Preserving You and Your Relationship in the Midst of Loss

Courageous Conversation: What do we do when our spouse, child(ren), best friends, parents, aunties, uncles etc. die and how does it impact our relationships?

Most relationships are challenged by death. It's not whether you or your relationship will struggle, it's how well will you struggle. Relationships can grow through the struggle of death which is a normal process in the cycle of life, but you will have to go deeper with your connection through prayer, meditation as well as your spiritual relationship in order to weather this particular storm. Joy comes in the morning; however, you may not know what morning it's coming. This too shall pass; it's just a matter of time. That said, we may not be as patient with the time frame required to heal from this kind of loss. Never the less, we must try to be patient with ourselves as well as our partners if we are grieving or if they are the ones grieving and we are charged to support them.

Trust the *process* of grief. They call it a *process* for a reason. There will be a roller coaster ride of emotions from anger, denial, bargaining, depression and finally acceptance. And in-between those emotions there may be many other emotional states that you don't quite understand.

Be patient with yourself and your partner. Your relationship may require a deeper level of faith. It's not whether you will make it through; it's how you will grow through this journey together as a couple. Our stress can be increased if we are grieving and cause us to displace our emotions onto the closest person to us. Remember, when death hits close to home, people often become more of who they are. Try to avoid having unrealistic expectations, especially if it requires others to do something different or unfamiliar.

There is power in the process of talking about death. The more we process our grief by talking about our experience the more palatable it becomes. Taking the risk to share your pain will only deepen your level of intimacy with your partner but it's hard.

If you are the support partner, be patient with your grieving spouse or confidant, letting them know you're there if they need you. Sometimes, there are no words that can ease the pain but the ministry of presence can comfort your grieving partner. Just knowing that someone is there to listen if they need to talk, need a hug or just need a shoulder to cry on can be comforting. With help, you and your relationship can not only survive but even thrive after a loved one has died. Keep in mind that thriving may require personal and relational work as you seek to grow through this challenging time. No matter how much you may think you are prepared for a loved one's transition, the process is still hard.

Grieving a loved one's death requires internal and external strength and fortitude. Try not to push away support unless you feel that it's not helpful or overwhelming to you or your family. Isolating is not always good for grief. Make sure you have multiple support systems to assist you during this difficult time. Be willing to ask for help even when you don't want to. You may have to discuss what changes need to be made with your lifestyle in order to weather the storm of death. Denial won't work; all relationships must adapt to change when someone close to us dies. The order to things, roles, rituals and habits will all shift in the aftermath of death.

Depression is normal when we go through this kind of difficulty but it's important to make sure you don't suffer in silence too long. Focus on honoring your loved one who has transitioned by vowing to live the life that they would want you to live purposefully and powerfully. This make take some time to get there so pace yourself over time. Pay attention to the frequency, intensity and longevity of your grief. This will give you and your partner a barometer for where you are in the process. Whether it's the first time you are experience this kind of loss or one of many experiences, no one grieves the same, so try to gradually grow through this experience while utilizing your partner or significant person in your life as a resource of comfort and support. This process is not meant to traverse in isolation so be kind to yourself and stay connected.

Call to Action: Begin externalizing your emotions by writing them in a journal. This will help you to track your progress while also preventing those toxic feelings from being bottled up inside your mind, body and spirit. Talk with your partner or confidant about your emotional state. Seek out grief therapy if your need it. It takes true strength not weakness to seek help. Just like there are rainbows on the other side of storms, you will grow through this and be stronger on the other side of your grief. This grief journey does not have to be the final chapter in your life. As you grow through this process, envision what your life and relationship will look like on the other side of your grief, then focus on getting to that mark.

Have a **beautiful day** on purpose from my heart to yours!

Journal Entry Date: _____

Courageous Action #39

_____

_____

_____

_____

Three Reasons Why This Is Significant for My Life:
Reason One: _____
Reason Two:_____
Reason Three:_____

What Will You Do With This Moment That
Allows It To Be Impactful For You and Others:

_____

_____

_____

_____

_____

What Courageous Conversation Can You Create
From This Action: _____

_____

_____

_____

_____

Week 40- FORGIVENESS: The Power to Let Go, the Courage to Forgive and the Freedom to Move on Courageously

Courageous Conversation: Everyone falls out with a family member, partner or friend now and again. Have you ever wondered why moving on from family or relationship drama and/or trauma is easier said than done?

Sometimes disagreements turn into long-term grudges with feelings of animosity, anger and resentment trumping love and familial and/or relational bonds. No matter the reason the problem began, you have been given the power to let go, the courage to forgive and the freedom to move on now, before it's too late.

At every stage of life, our relationships and families present us with both joys and challenges. Learning to manage stress, to understand our own emotions and behaviors, and to communicate effectively can help strengthen our own emotional health, as well as our connections to the important people in our lives.

Forgiveness is one of the hardest challenges that many of us will ever experience yet, I think many of you would agree with me that if you've ever forgiven or been forgiven, it's also one of the most rewarding and liberating experiences we could ever have.

Unforgiveness is often born out of pride, ego or fear, often causing us to remain in a holding pattern that can sabotage our very freedom to live our best lives. When we are unwilling and/or unable to forgive, we are also unable to let go and move on to become the best version of ourselves as human beings while fulfilling our divine assignment here on earth. In essence, unforgiveness has the power to cancel out our assignments, but forgiveness honors a more powerful principle leading us to share our *love, light, truth and accountability which ultimately leads to hope and freedom.*

I believe that most of us won't get through this life without being challenged to utter the words, I Forgive You or Please Forgive Me. At times, we may even have to learn to forgive ourselves for years of self-inflicted injuries which may then free us up to forgive those we love for their intentional or unintentional repeated injuries to us.

So, when we are pondering whether we should embark on that long and arduous journey of forgiveness, we must remember that we have the power to utilize the gift of forgiveness for ourselves and others. We need to remember a few things on this forgiveness journey:

- Forgiveness is a gift for our own freedom from the bondage of unforgiveness.
- Forgiveness is a process that takes time, so be patient with yourself and others.
- Forgiveness does not mean agreement or reconciliation; it simply means you no longer give unforgiveness power over your life.
- You can begin the journey of forgiveness by recognizing that we have all done something that is worthy of forgiveness, so perhaps incorporating the person you are angry with in your daily prayers and/or meditation can jump start the process.
- Envision the Emotional Freedom that you are embarking recognizing that the spirit of forgiveness affords you the opportunity to harness all the positive emotions that have been thwarted due to unforgiveness.
- Because Forgiveness is available, you already have the power to free yourself from unforgiveness and move on to living your best life, NOW!

Call to Action: Remember that we only have this short life here on this planet and it does not serve us well to stay stuck in anger, bitterness and resentment because we can't or won't let go. We can move beyond the hurt and pain caused by ourselves or someone else. That doesn't mean that we've forgotten or let them off the hook; it just means that we chose our own liberation over the residue of our past injuries. Join the freedom movement in embarking on the journey of forgiveness. Embrace the goal of growing through shame, fear & pride in order to experience the joy of landing on the other side with a spirit of faith, forgiveness, and freedom!

Have a **beautiful day** on purpose from my heart to yours!

Journal Entry Date: _____

Courageous Action #40

_____

_____

_____

_____

Three Reasons Why This Is Significant for My Life:

Reason One: _____

Reason Two:_____

Reason Three:_____

What Will You Do With This Moment That
Allows It To Be Impactful For You and Others:

_____

_____

_____

_____

_____

What Courageous Conversation Can You Create
From This Action: _____

_____

_____

_____

_____

CHAPTER 4
A Pathway to Living Your BEST Life NOW

Week 41- REST

Courageous Conversation: *Be Thankful* for the gift of REST. Why don't we rest more? What has happened in our culture that we believe REST is over rated?

These days, we don't give ourselves permission to REST, even though it is essential to our very being. Remember, the body keeps score and we are living in a world where our stress levels are through the roof and many of us find it hard to shift gears from our high intensity lives and just REST. Additionally, with the everyday grind required to simply sustain ourselves and our families, many are not in optimal positions to REST. Yet, it is rest that allows us to rejuvenate and restore for the next day, next journey, next experience; the good or bad fight and the next demotion or promotion. At a deep cellular level, our minds, bodies and spirits need rest to survive and thrive as we live out this thing called life.

In a world where multi-tasking, being overstimulated and over-functioning behaviors are usually the order of the day, simply getting the rest that your body deserves is a bit of an anomaly. With the busy lives that most of us live, it takes being intentional to rest. Sometimes, it's as simple as taking a walk to clear your head or eating lunch without distractions. Other times, finding time to rest requires much more thoughtfulness to execute on your own self-care. If you find yourself constantly fatigued and overwhelmed because you're burning the candle at both ends, give yourself permission to REST. Think about how it would feel to your mind, body and spirit to give yourself permission to exhale and rest on purpose. Intentionally decide to make rest a priority this year.

This decision will require that you don't say yes to everything and that you become more comfortable with saying no to certain requests. It will be hard at first because you may feel that you are missing out on something. That said, what good is it to make every event or occasion if you being unhealthy, fatigued and exhausted is the price you must pay. Take this challenge to infuse more rest into your life and in just a few weeks you may be surprised that you are much more productive and engaged after giving yourself permission to REST. When your mind is renewed, it allows your spirit to be restored and your body to be rejuvenated. Go for it...REST INTENTIONALLY on purpose and see what happens in the atmosphere.

Call to Action: Take necessary actions steps by making a commitment to do three things differently that will allow you to get more REST throughout the week. Keep a daily journal of your energy level, your productivity level and your level of social engagement. Then, enjoy the journey with REST as your vehicle to JOY.

Have a **beautiful day** on purpose from my heart to yours!

Journal Entry Date: _____

Courageous Action #41

_____

_____

_____

_____

Three Reasons Why This Is Significant for My Life:

Reason One: _____

Reason Two:_____

Reason Three:_____

What Will You Do With This Moment That
Allows It To Be Impactful For You and Others:

_____

_____

_____

_____

_____

What Courageous Conversation Can You Create
From This Action: _____

_____

_____

_____

_____

Week 42- JOY

Courageous Conversation: *Be Thankful* for the gift of JOY. Many people have lost their faith in JOY. Have you ever wondered why it appears that so many people are walking around joyless?

More and more, we encounter people in our day to day interactions whose primary emotions appear to be anger, sadness, despair, disappointment, frustration, bitterness and resentment. These emotions seem to be fueled by unresolved pain and a continuation of ongoing trauma. Emotional injuries will occur as a part of our lived and shared human experiences, yet there is JOY available to us on the other side of pain. We just have to remember that life is a continuum of good and bad experiences.

What if in the midst of pain, you encouraged yourself to harness the JOY deep down on the inside of you where no one can take it away. You see, as long as you are searching for external validation to fulfill your internal desire you will always be searching. But if you recognize that you have the power to hold on to your JOY, then you have the opportunity to experience life through an entirely different lens. While happiness is often based on what is happening, JOY is based on your internal relationship with you and the creator.

Therefore, no one can take the emotion of JOY away from you.

If you are thankful for every minute of the day, you can access your JOY in the journey. However, if you are like me, we can all be guilty of waiting for something big to happen. We are often so busy looking for that big moment, event or opportunity that we can't see the beauty of the forest for the trees.

You can choose to count every minute or make every minute count. Once you make that decision, you'll be open to the opportunity to count it all JOY; the ups, the downs and the in-betweens. Life is what you make it and how you experience the beauty of it depends on you. It's up to you to see the beauty in your own journey. Remember, if you woke up then you have another opportunity to experience your best life, many are not so blessed to awaken with another day here on earth. For some people, their minutes are cut short in life which reminds us that each day we are breathing is an opportunity to experience pure JOY.

Call to Action: Make a list of little and big things in the minutes, moments & memories you are blessed enough to experience. Remind yourself daily, if you have the gift of breath today then you are here on purpose so smile & experience JOY in your journey!

Have a **beautiful day** on purpose from my heart to yours!

Journal Entry Date: _____

Courageous Action #42

_____

_____

_____

_____

Three Reasons Why This Is Significant for My Life:

Reason One: _____

Reason Two:_____

Reason Three:_____

What Will You Do With This Moment That
Allows It To Be Impactful For You and Others:

_____

_____

_____

_____

_____

What Courageous Conversation Can You Create
From This Action: _____

_____

_____

_____

_____

Week 43- LOVE

Courageous Conversation: *Be Thankful* for LOVE and how it shows up internally and externally in your life. Have you ever asked yourself the question, if LOVE is free then why don't we experience the abundance of it more deeply and give it away more freely?

Let's talk about possessing the spirit of LOVE. In a world where there are so many images and reminders of hatred, it's important to remember to remind ourselves that LOVE *trumps hate.* Love is more infectious than hate and it triumphs over hate every time. If you find yourself moving towards the darker side of life due to life's circumstances, search deep inside for that part of yourself that you know is buried inside your heart. It is a universal truth that LOVE, light, truth and accountability equals hope and freedom. These are fundamental truths that we sometimes forget when it seems like darkness is permeating the atmosphere. Yet, the key to our happiness is right inside of us. We all hold the key to our own LOVE & Light and it's right there waiting for us to open the door to all of its endless possibilities for our lives.

Once you have access to it, you can harness it for the purpose of not only living your best life, but also for the purpose of treating people like they deserve to be treated. We all matter on this earth and the golden rule still has value; do unto others as you would have them do unto you. The truth is we all matter on this planet and there is enough LOVE to go around for all of us to enjoy while we're here on earth. Also, remember that you teach people how to treat you so if you're being treated in a manner that is less then you desire or deserve, it's time to LOVE yourself more and let go of those who don't value your worth.

As you think about who you LOVE, how you LOVE and the way you LOVE, focus on being intentional with giving and receiving LOVE abundantly. The spirit of LOVE is in all of us, you are no different, you just have to be willing to make a choice to express it both internally and externally. The universe will receive your LOVE and spread it to the world infectiously. You will be surprised at how LOVE comes back to you when you give it away freely.

Call to Action: LOVE is truly infectious and the more that you give it away freely, the more it returns back to you abundantly. LOVE is an action word. Make this the beginning of how you share, give and receive LOVE abundantly.

Make a list of all those you plan to give and show LOVE to starting with having a love affair with yourself and then offering the gift of LOVE through your actions to others. You won't regret giving it away freely, after all, it was already given to you freely from the beginning!

Have a **beautiful day** on purpose from my heart to yours!

Journal Entry Date: _____

Courageous Action #43

_____

_____

_____

_____

Three Reasons Why This Is Significant for My Life:

Reason One: _____

Reason Two:_____

Reason Three:_____

What Will You Do With This Moment That
Allows It To Be Impactful For You and Others:

_____

_____

_____

_____

_____

What Courageous Conversation Can You Create
From This Action: _____

_____

_____

_____

_____

Week 44- PEACE

Courageous Conversation: *Be Thankful* for the ability to access your PEACE from the inside out. Have you ever thought about where your PEACE is? Is it hiding in plane site or perhaps hiding in the shadows, unwilling to reveal itself to you?

Maybe your PEACE has been there all the time just waiting for you to say hello and embrace it as a familiar friend. We all have the ability to access those gifts that reside inside of us yet, we sometimes make choices to give our gifts away to those who don't value us the way we deserve to be valued.

It's important that you recognize the ways that you can harness your PEACE and protect it so that you can access it whenever you need it to relax, calm and prepare you for the next obstacle that comes your way. You have the ability to access your PEACE that surpasses all understanding which comes with the awareness that life can always be a lot worse.

There were two stories in the world news section. One was about a boy who had a degenerative disease where he would lose his eyesight in a year and he had a bucket list of places he wanted to see to create visual memories before he went totally blind. All this 12-year-old little boy wanted was to see Niagara Falls, the Grand Canyon, the Empire State building and as a sign of the times, the Google campus. The other thing he wanted was to see his favorite basketball team, the Boston Celtics play. I was so excited for him when I read that donors were helping him to live out his visual memory bucket list. Can you imagine having to have a bucket list at 12 years old? Most people look to create a bucket list when they are approaching their senior years.

Next, I read where a mom from North Carolina visiting Florida drove she, her three children and her unborn child into the ocean. Public citizens who saw what was happening rushed to their aid when they heard the screams of the children saying that their mom was trying to kill them. According to eyewitnesses, the mom just kept saying that they were okay as she turned the car towards the ocean and hit the gas pedal. Can you imagine being so distraught that you feel the only answer is to kill yourself and your four babies? They recued them but this story reminded me that we are all vulnerable to being in states of despair and sometimes need to be reminded that PEACE is inside of us; it has not departed from us.

I share these stories with you because if you're like me, there are just some days when things feel overwhelming and very challenging; like you just want a do-over for the day. However, it's usually not long before God reminds me of how blessed I truly am. Sometimes when we think things are bad, the universe reminds us that there are others that have it worse than us. When was a child, I remember my grandparents making statements in their prayers while thanking God for being in their right mind. I wasn't exactly sure what they were referring to then but now that I'm much older and have had a few lived and shared experiences under my belt, I know that they talking about having PEACE of mind. It's when you may not have all the answers but God still gives you that PEACE that surpasses all understanding. It's a wonderful gift that helps you sleep in the middle of the night even if things aren't going as you planned. PEACE reminds us, this too shall pass and you'll be fine.

My uncle Pat, my mother's youngest brother of nine children played professional baseball, retiring from the Baltimore Orioles. He then became an Evangelist Minister giving leadership to Lifeline Ministries by traveling all over the world preaching the gospel and his words remind me of my PEACE daily. He used to say, "if your pray don't worry and if you worry don't pray". I have learned that worry doesn't help, but prayer will give you PEACE that allows you to rest for the next leg of the journey. How about you?

***Call to Action:** If you woke up today grateful for the gift of sight through physical, spiritual and/or mental clarity and you realize that someone else out there in the universe is struggling more than you, be thankful for your PEACE and then use it to grow as you continue to learn more about yourself and others.*

Harness and protect your PEACE utilizing it to build your internal strength in preparation for the external challenges you are bound to face. Accessing your PEACE will absolutely help you to prepare for the hard times and appreciate the good times.

Have a **beautiful day** on purpose from my heart to yours!

Journal Entry Date: _____

Courageous Action #44

_____

_____

_____

_____

Three Reasons Why This Is Significant for My Life:

Reason One: _____

Reason Two:_____

Reason Three:_____

What Will You Do With This Moment That
Allows It To Be Impactful For You and Others:

_____

_____

_____

_____

_____

What Courageous Conversation Can You Create
From This Action: _____

_____

_____

_____

_____

Week 45- PREPARATION

Courageous Conversation: *Be Thankful* for the opportunity to PREPARE for what's next.

I always like to say, people don't plan to fail; they fail to plan. The question is not will opportunity come knocking at your door; the question is when opportunity comes knocking, will you be ready?

Most of us view certain times of the year as a time of reflection and renewal in order to restart the focus on some of our goals that we haven't quite completed yet. The truth is that we don't have to wait until any particular season rolls around; we can take action NOW. The opportunity for you to start preparing for your next level is today. Don't focus on doing tomorrow what you can prepare for today.

If not you, then who, if not NOW then when. Don't get caught up with your stinking thinking that tells you that it's too late, you're too old or your time is up. If you tell yourself these lies, they will become your truth but nothing could be further from the truth. Make a decision to reject the old tapes that have been renting free space in your head for far too long and start playing new tapes. Your best is truly yet to come but in order for it to come to fruition, you have to believe it, to conceive it and ultimately receive it!

Call to Action: There is no time like the present...Ready, set, grow!!!

*There is still time to focus our energy on making things happen and finishing out the year strong. Stay focused on preparing for your next level by making a decision to tie up loose ends, complete goals and finish the things that you started. Don't quit because it's too hard or because you get discouraged, those are the perfect times to **DIG DEEP**... Prepare, then go for it and tell yourself that it's time to execute to in order to **WIN**. You have nothing to lose and everything to gain so what are you waiting for? **Let Go, Let God and Let's Go....***

Have a **beautiful day** on purpose from my heart to yours!

Journal Entry Date: _____
Courageous Action #45

_____
_____
_____
_____

Three Reasons Why This Is Significant for My Life:
Reason One: _____
Reason Two:_____
Reason Three:_____

What Will You Do With This Moment That
Allows It To Be Impactful For You and Others:

_____
_____
_____
_____
_____

What Courageous Conversation Can You Create
From This Action: _____

_____
_____
_____
_____

Week 46- RELATIONSHIPS

Courageous Conversation: *Be Thankful* for knowing the difference between Seasonal versus Lifer RELATIONSHIPS.

It's important to recognize the value of your seasonal relationships as well as your lifer relationships. Be thankful for the ability to know the difference. Too often we put our relationships in the wrong category. I for one have found myself guilty of being in denial and resisting the reality that many of my relationships I thought were for a lifetime, where in fact only for a season. I had to face the harsh reality that those relationships had to end in order for new ones to begin.

It's also important for us to realize that there are some things we want and can't have and some things we have and don't want. Relationships often fall into the category of a constantly changing organism. If we're unable or unwilling to accept changes in our relationships, we may find ourselves stuck holding on to something that was never meant to last forever. Acceptance is the key to adapting to transitions in our relationships. Once we accept the purpose the relationships serve in our lives, whether it's our spouse, our friends, our family members etc., then we determine the relationships' impact on our wellbeing and ultimately what needs to change.

Call to Action: Focus on your discerning spirit that allows you to know when it's over or to know when you need to fight to maintain the relationships that matter most. The spirit will move you in the direction of when to hold on and when to let go. Listen carefully, be still or take action based on your internal guide post.

Have a **beautiful day** on purpose from my heart to yours!

Journal Entry Date: _____

Courageous Action #46

_____

_____

_____

_____

Three Reasons Why This Is Significant for My Life:
Reason One: _____

Reason Two:_____

Reason Three:_____

What Will You Do With This Moment That
Allows It To Be Impactful For You and Others:

_____

_____

_____

_____

_____

What Courageous Conversation Can You Create
From This Action: _____

_____

_____

_____

_____

Week 47- FRIENDSHIPS

Courageous Conversation:

Be Thankful for the gift of FRIENDSHIPS for life. Many are not so blessed to have true friendships that last a lifetime. If you are reading this entry it's time to talk about lifers.

Let's be thankful for the beauty of our long-term lifetime friendships. If you are fortunate enough to have a friend who has journeyed with you throughout life then celebrate it. Some people only have seasonal friendships that don't stand the test of time. Many of us keep these friends in our lives far beyond their expiration date due to loyalty, longevity or legacy.

Conversely, if you have the opportunity to be blessed by a lifelong friend, tell them that you're thankful for who they represent in your life. Sometimes, our friends become our family; I like to call them FRAMILY. There are some friends we have for a season, a reason or a lifetime. Yet, if we are privileged enough to have a few friends in the world that we know without a shadow of a doubt will be in our lives through a lifetime of milestones with the ups and downs, this is truly something to be thankful for. Lifer friendships are gifts that make our place in the world feel more secure so enjoy them as you share life's journey together.

Call to Action: Make a decision to not keep friends in your life past their expiration date. Have a courageous conversation that's gracious yet deliberate in letting go of toxic friends who do not add value to your life and have proven to impact your life in negative and unhealthy ways. Next, celebrate your healthy friendships by being intentional about sharing quality time with one of your lifer friends this year. When you connect, take the time to let them know how much you appreciate their presence in your life. It shouldn't be taken for granted when we have beautiful friendships that we know will be with us through the highs and lows; the good and bad; and for better and worse. These are our chosen family and for that we should be truly thankful.

Have a **beautiful day** on purpose from my heart to yours!

Journal Entry Date: _____

Courageous Action #47

_____

_____

_____

_____

Three Reasons Why This Is Significant for My Life:
Reason One: _____

Reason Two:_____

Reason Three:_____

What Will You Do With This Moment That
Allows It To Be Impactful For You and Others:

_____

_____

_____

_____

_____

What Courageous Conversation Can You Create
From This Action: _____

_____

_____

_____

_____

Week 48- TESTS

Courageous Conversation: *Be Thankful* for the TEST; with no TEST there is no testimony.

Any test that comes your way is not just to frustrate you or make you sad; most tests come with multiple lessons and testimonies along the way. The question is not whether you will go through tests, trials and tribulations; the question that should resonate most in your spirit is how will your grow through the difficult times that test your faith and use the process and the outcome as a testimony to bless others. Your mess can truly become your message, you just have to make a decision to stay connected to your faith. My good friend and husband's spiritual father Gene A. Jefferson, always tells me, FEAR and FAITH can never reside in the same place. The choice is yours to choose one or the other.

Simply trusting your spiritual connection to see you through the test allows you to grow in the midst of the experience. All circumstances are simply, experiences that shape you along the way. These tests are meant to strengthen you for the next leg of the journey. God will always see you through the test, not because of you but in spite of you. Changing your perspective will allow you to view your tests differently as the new you, emerges.

Call to Action: Make a list of all the things you've been tested by in life and the ways you grew through those experiences. Now you have data to prove that you are not just a survivor but a person that is destined to thrive. Remember, the TEST is to prepare you for the game days of life. Focus on what you are supposed to learn about yourself and then tell yourself; it's only a TEST, but my testimony is gonna be a blessing to many.

Have a **beautiful day** on purpose from my heart to yours!

Journal Entry Date: _____

Courageous Action #48

_____

_____

_____

_____

Three Reasons Why This Is Significant for My Life:

Reason One: _____

Reason Two:_____

Reason Three:_____

What Will You Do With This Moment That
Allows It To Be Impactful For You and Others:

_____

_____

_____

_____

_____

What Courageous Conversation Can You Create
From This Action: _____

_____

_____

_____

_____

Week 49- STORMS

Courageous Conversation: *Be Thankful* for the STORMS in your life because without STORMS there would be no RAINBOWS.

Have you ever wondered what the purpose of storms are? In the natural realm, storms clear the atmosphere from all the toxins in the environment. In our personal and spiritual realm, storms are meant to correct, constrict, connect or change us. Most of us are in the middle of a storm, moving out of a storm or moving into a storm. The wonderful thing about storms is that they don't last forever. Storms do end and in the aftermath of the storm, we need to evaluate what we gained from that particular storm so that we can use the lessons learned for the next storm in our lives.

If you live long enough, you will have multiple storms in your life but this also means that you will have multiple rainbows in your life as well. Rainbows come out after storms to give you hope that a new day is coming. Be strong enough to not give up and courageous enough to rebuild what was lost as you move on to create something better for yourself and for those you love. Take what you've learned about yourself from that storm and make the appropriate course corrections to guide you to your next level. You are stronger than you realize.

Call to Action: Make a list of the various storms you've been through and how you made the appropriate corrections, constrictions, connections or changes. This will not only give you greater awareness of how strong you truly are, but it will also clear those obstacles out of your life in order to make room for new energy and new vision as you rebuild, repurpose and reposition yourself to receive the spirit of abundance in your new life NOW!

Have a **beautiful day** on purpose from my heart to yours!

Journal Entry Date: _____

Courageous Action #49

_____

_____

_____

_____

Three Reasons Why This Is Significant for My Life:

Reason One: _____

Reason Two:_____

Reason Three:_____

What Will You Do With This Moment That
Allows It To Be Impactful For You and Others:

_____

_____

_____

_____

_____

What Courageous Conversation Can You Create
From This Action: _____

_____

_____

_____

_____

Week 50- PAIN to POWER

Courageous Conversation: *Be Thankful* for the PAIN; it's in the PAIN that we begin to understand the beauty of the ability to turn PAIN into POWER.

You might ask me what's that about Dr. Argie; why would anyone be thankful for pain? Well, I'm glad you asked, you see when you think about it, most of us don't experience gain without pain. Whether it's our workout regimen, studying hard to complete an academic program, raising our children or simply working hard to accomplish a well sought out goal; none of it comes without pain in some shape or form. Most of us would like to avoid the pain and enjoy the gain. Unfortunately, the universe doesn't always align with that philosophy. There is a reason why those who have been through painful experiences have such power on the other side of their journey…it's called grace and inspiration.

It's been stated that those who appreciate life the most are those who have experienced the most pain. The truth is that most of us will endure a measure of pain in our lives but the question is, will the pain we experience reveal the strength of our faith or the lack of it. The choice is yours to use the pain as a weapon to hurt others because you hurt or to turn your pain into power and use it to elevate others as well as launch your own elevation. You choose!

Call to Action: Make a decision to turn your pain into power by being thankful for the lessons learned and the faith building experience. After all, how do you really know how great God is unless you've been through a storm and made it to the other side. Make pain your purpose as a vehicle to your power.

Have a **beautiful day** on purpose from my heart to yours!

Journal Entry Date: _____

Courageous Action #50

_____

_____

_____

_____

Three Reasons Why This Is Significant for My Life:

Reason One: _____

Reason Two:_____

Reason Three:_____

What Will You Do With This Moment That
Allows It To Be Impactful For You and Others:

_____

_____

_____

_____

_____

What Courageous Conversation Can You Create
From This Action: _____

_____

_____

_____

_____

Week 51- STRETCH

Courageous Conversation: *Be Thankful* for the ability to STRETCH yourself beyond the capacity you ever thought possible.

Even when you think you have nothing left in the tank and no more energy to expend; your spiritual connection will give you more internal strength in order for you to be an external blessing. Stretching yourself requires that you first engage in radical self-care. This is a both/and process; not and either-or process. Stretching yourself as you prepare for whatever fight comes your way whether it be a new relationship that you want to succeed or a lost opportunity you felt was unjustly taken; it all requires that you put your OXYGEN MASK on first and breath in energy in order to maintain the stretch that is required for you to WIN.

The POWER you have, not just external power but internal power will help you in your STRETCH. What do I mean? If you are reading this entry, I hope you would agree that there is another type of power that is hard to shut down. This is the kind of power that no weapon formed against it will prosper. You have the internal power that resides inside of you and allows you to know that no matter what obstacles come your way, your internal strength will overcome it. Realizing that you have been given infinite internal power allows you to seek refuge while being protected from all the external disruptions, distractions & deceptions. No matter what the situation looks like on the outside, remember that God has given us infinite power on the inside.

Call to Action: Take a look in the mirror daily and tell yourself that you are powerful beyond measure. Remind yourself throughout the day of how it feels to be powerful even as you are stretching yourself beyond your capacity. You are stronger than you think. Your STRETCH will quantum leap you to your next level. So, breath in, breath out and take action to live you best life now...YOU GOT THIS!!!

Have a **beautiful day** on purpose from my heart to yours!

Journal Entry Date: _____

Courageous Action #51

_____

_____

_____

_____

Three Reasons Why This Is Significant for My Life:

Reason One: _____

Reason Two: _____

Reason Three: _____

What Will You Do With This Moment That
Allows It To Be Impactful For You and Others:

_____

_____

_____

_____

_____

What Courageous Conversation Can You Create
From This Action: _____

_____

_____

_____

_____

Week 52- ENOUGH

Courageous Conversation: *Be Thankful* that you are more than ENOUGH!!!

We have many messages in the world that offer the narrative that we aren't good enough and that we have nothing to offer, but the truth is, if you are here, then you are here on purpose. Yet, it's not enough for others to believe that you are ENOUGH, you have to own your own real estate and believe that you are more than ENOUGH. Once you make this transformation, you will begin to live your limitless life with less fear and with unlimited expectation and anticipation of your next levels. Here's a few things that will help you on your pathway to living your **Best Life** Now:

Stop apologizing for staying in your own lane

Embrace the ability to stay in your own lane and focus on the greatest competition of all; competition with yourself. Each day, wake up with the realization that you have another opportunity to make a difference in your corner of the world. Smile early in the morning and often throughout the day at the thought of you blazing a path that makes sense out of non-sense for you to WIN while living your *BEST LIFE* now.

Remember, too often you will find that it's so easy to look at what others have acquired or what they are accomplishing and wish that it was you. Fight the urge to compare yourself to others. It's important to think about the fact that if the grass seems greener on the other side of the street, it may be time to water our own grass.

When you are truly happy for other people's successes as well as their blessings it will help you to know without a shadow of a doubt that your blessings are available in abundance. Don't hate; celebrate and then create a pathway to living your best life on purpose.

Strengthen Your Health: Mind, Body and Spirit

Be thankful for a healthy body. Several years ago, I made a decision to focus on physical and mental clarity in my life so I started a 3-day cleanse. I didn't have much confidence that I could do it in the beginning but each day I began to feel stronger mentally, physically and spiritually growing more confident in myself and my spiritual connection. I never felt hungry or deprived, but my body started feeling refreshed, renewed and revived. The spiritual clarity was amazing and my body felt strong and clean on the inside and outside.

Encourage yourself to make a decision to take care of your vessel. If you spend a lot of time giving your resources away then you need to think about ways to replenish your mind, body and spirit internally and externally. Don't forget to treat yourself like the precious gift that you are. In doing so you will not just be blessed, but you will be a blessing to others just in your ordinary walk for an extraordinary purpose.

Breath, Inhale, Exhale, Release & Celebrate YOU

Be thankful for the ability to breath. It starts from there by simply slowing things down and inhaling, then exhaling. Feel the release of all the energy. Breath in good energy and breath out negative energy.

Life moves so fast that like most people, you may sometimes feel like you're a hamster on a wheel. Be mindful that if you don't take the time to exhale it won't happen. You really can't help others to reach their level of excellence, whether it's your kids, spouse, parents or friends when you are completely depleted. Yet, they will expect you to anyway. Thus, it's up to you to be intentional about taking the time to exhale while working your own radical self-care as a priority.

In the stressful days to come, give yourself permission to take a moment to just breath and celebrate that you're still standing. Based on what you've been through, you are worth celebrating. Embrace this beautiful day in the moment and make a decision to pace yourself without rushing. If you don't take excellent care of yourself, no one else will. So, whatever you do, find some time to take excellent care of YOU as you level-up. You're going to need to be healthy in every area of your life for the journey you are embarking on.

Embrace Living Your BEST Life Now on Purpose

Be thankful for the people who have touched your life on purpose in ways that have made a difference and for the lives that you've touched on purpose that have made a difference as well. It's all about creating bridges not barriers within our connections to humanity. Too often, we are unaware of how our actions impact others. Most days we're all so busy with the hustle and bustle of life that we tend to miss out on what really matters most; our human connections from one heart to the next.

If you are like me, you have had wonderful friends and/or family members that show up like Angels just at the right time. We never know who God will place in our lives, but sometimes we have to just trust that he has a plan for us and our relationships.

Once I was able to let go of unhealthy relationships, I was able to make space for healthy relationships. How about you? Don't keep people in your life way beyond their expiration date. Once you make room, God will fill that space with Angels that are ready, willing and able to journey with you to your next level. Also, while you're going to your next level, make a decision to be kind to yourself first, offering yourself love, care, kindness, good will, affirmation, acknowledgement and acceptance. Filling yourself up will give you the overflow you need to share your gifts in abundance with others versus constantly giving from your deficit.

Finally, prayer, preparation, permission and promise can move you into position by creating a pathway to live your Best Life on PURPOSE. By stepping outside your comfort zone and intentionally re-setting your mindset, you are now in position to take the necessary risks to receive EPIC WINS. Why play small and sit on the sidelines of life, when you can play big and get in the game. By embarking on this journey, you've already won and the best is yet to come.

Call to Action: Give yourself permission to live your life with no excuses, intentional wellbeing and extraordinary experiences. Remember, you have nothing to lose and everything to gain, so what are you waiting for? It's up to YOU to write the next chapter(s) of your life; why not start by writing the most amazing prelude to Living Your BEST Life Now on Purpose! Go for it, I can't wait to see you on the other side of your elevation as you walk into your greatness! Your DESTINY is waiting ...Let Go, Let God and Let's Go.....

Have a **beautiful day** on purpose from my heart to yours!

Journal Entry Date: _____
Courageous Action #52

_____
_____
_____
_____

Three Reasons Why This Is Significant for My Life:
Reason One: _____
Reason Two:_____
Reason Three:_____

What Will You Do With This Moment That
Allows It To Be Impactful For You and Others:

_____
_____
_____
_____
_____

What Courageous Conversation Can You Create
From This Action: _____

_____
_____
_____
_____